Marc's back with tons more to inspire you with! It's clear that Marc wrote this book to remind you that you've got a friend in the business of creating your future, and that you have everything you need within you to get it done. He's got more stories and advice that are full of energy, never boring, and will literally change the way your brain is wired to create limitless possibilities!

- Tara M Ruttley, PhD- Neuroscientist, Space Scientist and TedX Speaker

"Your consistency is what creates your results." Wow, these words are true to success at all levels!

- Robert Kofroth, 2018 NASKA (North American Sport Karate Association) World Champion

Once again Marc is provocative, on point and unapologetic, as he pushes and prods the reader to look within themselves; his rants are blasts of uncontrolled energy that hit you between the eyes, forcing you to look deeper into yourself.

- Honorable Michael Cabry, President Of Special Court Judges Of Pennsylvania

Hayford's book feels like a friend, the best kind of friend, who understands you in your low points and fills you with energy to lift yourself up. Personal and familiar, this friend helps you discover what is possible in your life.

- Katey Forth, PhD, World Champion Professional Ultimate Frisbee Player, CEO & Founder of ZIBRIO

Marc Hayford!!! WOW! He has the energy and positivity that can get you through any challenge.

- Dr. Darren Rodia, Founder & CEO of Kinetic Physical Therapy (2015's #1 American Physical Therapy Practice Of The Year)

Marc Hayford will take you to another place if you'll let him. And it's a place you want to go. If you're down or just needing a boost - read this book! It's quick but powerful.

- Angie Cella, 2020 Toy Inventor Of The Year & "Blinger" Creator

# LIGHT UP THE
# DARKNESS

**MARC HAYFORD**

Light Up The Darkness

2020 by Marc Hayford

Published by Publisher Name

All rights reserved. No part of this publication may be reproduced, distributed, or transmitted in any form or by any means, including photocopying, recording, or other electronic or mechanical methods, without the prior written permission of the publisher, except in the case of brief quotations embodied in critical reviews and certain other noncommercial uses permitted by copyright law. For permission requests, write to the publisher, addressed "Attention: Permissions Coordinator," at the address below.

Printed in the United States of America
ISBN: 9798657714074

First Edition
10 9 8 7 6 5 4 3 2 1

# TABLE OF
# CONTENTS

Acknowledgments – 1

Let There Be Light – 4

Rant 1: *Right Now* – 8
Key #1 – **MINDSET (Focus On What You Want)** – 11

Rant 2: *Raw Warning* – 22
Key #2 – **ATTITUDE (Lose The Loser)** – 27

Rant 3: *Daydream Breakthrough* – 41
Key #3 – **VISION (See It To Be It)** – 44

Rant 4: *Repetition* – 56
Key #4 – **DISCIPLINE (Work Ethic Wins)** – 61

Rant 5: *Control* – 77
Key #5 – **MOTIVATION (High Energy)** – 81

Rant 6: *Get Moving* – 89
Key #6 – **COURAGE (Hacking Fear)** – 92

Rant 7: *Shhhh* – 107
KEY #7 – **UNREALISTIC (Get Crazy)** – 111

Rant 8: *Humility* – 121
KEY #8 – **GRATITUDE (Happy To Be Here)** – 124

Rant 9: *Forgive* – 132
KEY #9 – **FAITH (The Power Of Belief)** – 134

I Believe – 144

About The Author – 146

# ACKNOWLEDGEMENTS

**ALL MY WORK** has always been dedicated to my family. Christina, Kane, Jayda and Harrison: I am so thankful for the time that I have been blessed with to be husband and father for this family. You are always my driving force. In addition, this particular labor of love is dedicated to those who shouldered the weight of what the year 2020 has brought us on a global scale.

To the class of 2020: I am truly sorry that you never had the chance to dance at your senior prom. I am heartbroken that you didn't get your final season in spring sports, or feel what it was like to coast in the last quarter of your last year of required schooling—in a classroom. Together. For those affected, I am crushed that you never had the chance to walk that stage at the graduation that didn't take place. Stay strong and know that even though it doesn't feel like it, your life is only just beginning. You missed out on a moment, but this is a marathon, not a sprint. Your future is BRIGHT.

I wrote this for all the brides to be, their soon to be husbands, and immediate family who had to deal with the concern of what was supposed to be your special day. The struggle of juggling vendors, venues, guests, schedules, finances, and everything else has added stress and stolen some magic from what was set to be one of the greatest days of your life. I know you've been dreaming about it for a lifetime. I'm sure you've had, or are going to have your big day, and that it was or will be simply amazing. Just realize that the partner you have, the lifetime ahead of both of you, and the memories that you are going to create is what is most important. If you can forgive, listen, and love, nobody can ever take that away. The best is yet to come.

All those young men and women who trained their whole life to entertain us and compete for a once in a lifetime opportunity to forever be an Olympic athlete has been put on ice. We won't be able to cheer for you just yet, and I am sorry. I can't wait for the moment when we can.

As I write, my heart extends itself to the entertainers, small business owners, independent consultants, entrepreneurs, and everyone else who felt numb with fear. Your livelihood and means of taking care of yourself and the ones you love was threatened or ripped away with uncertainty of how and when you could ever make ends meet. Wondering how you can make it to the next paycheck or if there will even be a next paycheck is heavy. Trust and BELIEVE that things will get better. If you keep failing forward and taking another step just like you have before, it will.

Equally for those that had no work, this is dedicated to those who did. Doctors, nurses, store workers, police, restaurant employees, essential personnel, and everyone else who had to fight through unsettling times have all opened our eyes. You went through some rough patches being asked not just to do your jobs, but to immediately do them differently, with more difficulty so you can ensure safety for yourself and others. You forever more will be looked upon with gratitude.

Having the feeling of no control is hard. Cyber schooling your kid when you never signed up to do so is hard. Being the kid who suddenly now has to relearn how to learn and do cyber school is hard. Not knowing what tomorrow will bring is hard. Fear, uncertainty, and lack of faith is hard. Taking the next step is hard. Getting out of bed is hard. Getting out of bed is especially hard when you have no place to go.

I wrote this for those who have felt the "hard." We're all on this ride together. We are battle tested and will rise again. We're going to have dark times, but we will have times of sunshine, too.

You reading this is not a happy accident. This book found you, and it was written for you. My intention is that it lights up your darkness.

# LET THERE BE LIGHT

*"What is to give light must endure burning" - Viktor Frankl*

**BEFORE TAKING THIS** journey together, I wanted to share a quick story with you. As an author it is obviously important to connect with the reader. Here my intent is to give you the authentic background as to how, why, and when "*Light Up The Darkness*" was created. I believe having a "behind the scenes" look will not only help you become part of this experience, but ultimately have a deeper appreciation for the heart and soul of it's inception. What you are about to read is the actual account of how #LUTD came into existence. I hope you enjoy it.

The framework of what I thought was going to be my 3rd book was on ice. My editor Kayla had thoughts on revamping portions of it. Christina (my wife, closest advocate, chief strategist—and let's face it—one who wants me to win the most) felt it failed in comparison to my first release "*Get Up*."

I was stunned. I thought I was on my way to releasing the next "*Grapes Of Wrath*," or "*To Kill A Mockingbird*" while the collective opinion of my chosen inner circle was that this unknown masterpiece was less to be desired. Despite the dissent of this particular and, select group of my choosing, I felt they were entitled to their opinion. Even if I thought their opinion was wrong.

What made me pump the brakes wasn't the fact that I was swayed by bad reviews, because I wasn't. What made me pump the brakes was the fact (as my wife pointed out) that the population of earth was creeping towards 8 billion people, and not one percent of them had the opportunity to be introduced to my first two books. Why even consider releasing a third book so soon? There was more work to do with what I've already created. Made sense.

So, I planned. I scheduled. I networked. I worked it. I was grinding. Book signings, speaking events, and steps to continue promotion for the first two books were filling the calendar.

The universe? Well, the universe had other ideas. One of my favorite lyrics from a John Lennon song reads "Life's what happens while you're busy making other plans." God chuckles at our monumental intended plans especially when it compares to his overall big picture.

The new decade hit, and with it, 2020 brought the pandemic of COVID-19, the coronavirus. Planet earth was put in an unexpected timeout on a global level like never seen before.

All those speaking events? All of those book signings? All of those school assemblies? The tours? Postponed. Cancelled. Wiped out. Rescheduled to who knows when.

The creation of *"LIGHT UP THE DARKNESS"* came to me appropriately in the dead of night when I was awakened to a silent household. Everyone was peaceful and asleep and I was perplexed as to why I was completely awake in the middle of the night like one would be in the middle of the day. I was literally wide awake. After laying there for what seemed like forever, I came to the realization that in my lifetime most of my ideas and creations that have fostered success have come to me in hours like this. And then it hit me. Get Up.

So I did. I literally raced to my computer and wrote down what I believed could be the key principles for myself, my family, my friends, the people I care about, and anyone willing to read my work. I wrote down nine underlining key fundamentals for success. These are what I believe will become a blueprint to use, not just to help fight back during dark days, but to win with, and ultimately, keep you winning in all circumstances. The key attributes are:

1) Mindset
2) Attitude
3) Vision
4) Discipline
5) Motivation
6) Courage
7) Being Unrealistic
8) Gratitude
9) Faith

When I sat there, my jaw dropped as I again was reminded that success does not come in our time, but God's time. All of these key principles were already outlined chapters of what I intended to be a completely different variation of my third book. Those chapters have now become "keys," and each "key" will be it's own dedicated chapter here. What I envisioned would have been great had it been released when I originally wanted. But, this? This message? Delivered now? This isn't great. This is a necessity.

I got to work quickly as adjustments needed to be made. Additions needed to be created and more fire—much more fire was mandatory if this was going to be powerful enough for the current times we are living in.

I know *"LIGHT UP THE DARKNESS"* will serve you well, because as I mentioned in the acknowledgments, you didn't pick it up by accident. And I want you to remember something: When you have great times, bad times can come; so prepare before you need to. When you have bad times, great times will come; so hang on because those great times are on the way.

Hemingway once said, "Writing is easy: all you have to do is sit down with a typewriter and bleed." Well, I don't have a typewriter. I have a MacBook. But I'm about to shed great amounts of blood. For you.

Keep fighting. Keep reading. Let's Light it up.

- Marc

## RANT #1

# RIGHT NOW

> "The Great Depression was a blessing in disguise. It reduced the whole world to a new staring point that gave everyone a new opportunity."
> – Napoleon Hill, *Think And Grow Rich*

**THE INTERNET IS** a hot mess when it comes to false, misquoted memes. We live in the "information age," but information doesn't always mean the truth. "The problem with quotes found on the internet is that they are often not true" said Abraham Lincoln never.

One particular meme that pops up now and again seems to have a profound message with convincing conviction. You've seen it. Whether the picture is of Charlie Brown and Snoopy sitting on a pier staring out into the ocean, the character "Dwight" from "The Office," or even the confident, smiling Buddha himself, the picture reads, "You only live once. Wrong! You only die once. You live every day."

Well, that's wrong. Simply existing is not living. Not taking advantage of the life that you were given is wasteful. Sucking the magic out of today and right now with worrying about tomorrow is actually a slow death. You can quote me. I approve of this message.

So that brings us to now. The "Roaring 20's!" They're here. Again. That's exciting to me. I hope it's still exciting to you, too. What will you do with this new start? What kind of moves will you make in this fresh decade? Despite stumbling out of the gates and how it's been otherwise advertised, this decade is wide open, stacked, and jammed packed with possibilities.

Opportunity is everywhere. You are alive! You must have your head out of the sand and your eyes WIDE open. I'm sure this next chapter of life will have both advances and obviously, as we've seen from the get go, setbacks. Ultimately, how you handle them will define you. Former British Prime Minister Winston Churchill said "For myself I am an optimist—it does not seem to be much use being anything else." There probably aren't too many times that negative thinking brought you happiness or success. It's time for all of us to be aware of our thoughts and feelings and be in charge of them. You are in the driver's seat and it is time for you to take control of life instead of life taking control of you.

Not all of us have equal talents but we all have equal opportunity to seek opportunities and create a better future for ourselves. We have more knowledge, access, information, and capabilities than ever before. Despite what we've been hearing and what we've been told, we can leave this place better than how we've found it.

Don't dismiss what you perceive as failure; it may be a blessing. Don't shut down if you don't get exactly what you want; maybe rejection is your divine protection. Don't check out when something is taken from you; maybe this creates an opportunity for your hands to be free to receive something bigger and better.

When our planet went into a global shut down, each scheduled event to event to event was cancelled right from underneath me. When this happened, things became quiet for not just the world, but for *my* world. THAT is exactly the moment when I was able to build from ground zero and create the very book you are reading right now.

This is a call to action! This is a fresh start. This is a chance for you to live your best life now by simply thinking bigger and deciding to be more unbiased than ever before. The times are changing again, and the good news is you can too. You are able and ready to evolve and grow, you simply need to choose it.

They told us that we needed to practice social distancing. We didn't. We practiced physical distancing, but socially? We may have grown closer than we ever have before. Families have had dinners together again. Zooms and "Facetimes" kept businesses, friends, and loved ones connected. Instead of having birthday parties, children had full birthday parades given by some of their favorite people.

You are living in the greatest time in the history of history. You are still young enough to do and old enough to know. You are alive! Decide to use this great gift. Let's start realizing that life really is happening for us, not to us. You are not a victim. You are a winner, and all you have to do is claim your prize.

# KEY 1
# MINDSET (FOCUS ON WHAT YOU WANT)

*"I look at this game from a different perspective."* —Pitbull

**WHEN YOU GET** done with this book, I want you to feel like a billion bucks. And, I hope you're as excited to read this first chapter as I was to write it. I am white hot and passionate about this first key subject. It's a simple concept, and although so powerful, maybe it's too simple as I see so many who get tripped up by it.

I look at it like this: if you're going to bother to put in the work, you might as well be great at doing it. And, if you are going to read this book, I need to make your time count. The foremost important thought we need to cover before we explore anything further, is that we all need to start focusing more on what we *do* want, and less on what we *don't* want. This is imperative!

Simple, right? Sure.

Easy? Well, you'd be surprised. Most people act like an extra in their own life's movie when the fact of the matter is they should be striving for the academy award. Check this out...

> *"When the student is ready, the teacher will appear. When the student is truly ready...the teacher will disappear."* — Tao Te Ching

I was working with a young man who was about to enter a D1 college with a scholarship for football. He was fast as lightning but considered grossly undersized. We were discussing mindset and what it would look like for him to create his own success.

"Yeah, yeah, I know," he reassured me. "I spoke with my uncle. He was telling me how I have a good thing going and not to screw around and mess it up. He told me not to do anything stupid. So, I'm good."

Oh my.

That was the first problem. He was so not "good." Not if he was looking to exceed expectations—which is exactly where his energy should have been flowing and what he should have been focusing on. "Not mess it up?" Yuck. "Don't do anything stupid?" Wrong answer. You don't exceed expectations by "not messing it up." You exceed expectations by going above and beyond what the herd is willing to do. And many times the herd—*that* status quo?

Well, that group is focusing on "not messing it up." Winners should focus on winning.

Instead of focusing on "not screwing around" and "not messing it up," why don't we focus on what it is going to take to be a standout and get onto the field? Why don't we start looking at doing what the other 98% will not do so we can trend towards being in that top 2%? Why don't we focus on regimented sleep, a purposeful diet, and specific workouts that will lend to strength and possibly bulking while not foregoing that speed that opened the potential door of success in the first place? How about we add an additional solid hour of film and playbook time, leaving the other twenty three hours for the other necessities like practice, school, sleep and life?

Doesn't that sound a little more on purpose than "not screwing around?" "Not messing it up" should never even enter the realm of conversation. If it does, it should be dismissed as a joke that is immediately cast out of the mind. Why? Because that mindset will not breed success. By focusing on what we DO want—not what we DON'T want—all those crucial little details of success, that most will not be willing to do, is what can get this aspiring-playmaking hopeful a shot to do just that: make plays.

Too many times we are out here in the game of life trying not to lose when we should be focusing on what it takes to win. I was beyond telling him to not do anything stupid. I was telling him to stretch himself and to go for it.

*"For the thing which I greatly feared has come upon me, and that which I was afraid of is come unto me."* — Job 3:25

I'm going to be very lucid here. I have belief in you like most other people don't. I may believe in you more than you actually believe in yourself. I know we are all capable of amazing, extraordinary, unrealistic things but I believe in order for that to manifest, there has to be a minding of our minds. We all carry an energy or a vibration, and it needs to be raised.

We must take control of our own thoughts. Let's stop putting in our minds the opposite of what we want, and let's start leaning in towards what we do want. We need to start becoming hypersensitive to our thoughts, our words, and our emotions because they all have power, and our subconscious mind is working even when we aren't.

You play on a frequency, like a radio station. Whether you like it, realize it, care about it or not, you are tuned in. But what are you tuning into? You need to be careful because you are going to get what you are looking for. If you are expecting good, you're going to find it. If you're expecting bad, you're going to find that too. Are you expecting success, or are you hoping that the wheels don't fall off? I'm not talking about blind, wishful thinking. I'm talking about mindset!

If you are listening to music on the radio and you tune into the classic rock station, you may hear Led Zeppelin, The Who, or Queen. You won't hear Mozart, Bach, or Beethoven there. That's on the classical music station. And you won't hear the work of Mozart, Bach, or Beethoven on the current pop station. In the year 2020 that's where you'll get Post Malone, Drake, and maybe Billie Eilish. Don't even think about hearing this week's number one song on the oldies station either, because that's where you can catch "Good Vibrations" by the Beach Boys.

That powerful asset—your brain—works the same way. Think of your mind as the radio receiver that tunes into frequencies. Ever get a new car and all of a sudden you see that exact same make and model car that you are driving is now everywhere? In reality, those cars have been there the whole time, but now you're just noticing them more because you're in tune with them. Well, this concept works exactly like that. Be specific when tuning into your channel.

> *"Losers visualize the penalties of failure. Winners visualize the rewards of success"* — Kobe Bryant

I'm into accentuating positives. When you dwell on inferior you become inferior. When you have a scarcity mindset, how can you grow? When you think about losing, how can you win? Instead of asking yourself "Why me?" Start asking yourself "Why not me?" Better yet, maybe start telling yourself "It is me!"

We need to stop listening to the negativity that we may not even realize we are being fed everyday. It drags us down. Music, television and the internet all want us to NEED something. When we think we are in a state of lack, we become anxious. When we become anxious, we become desperate. When we get desperate, we become dependent. And *they* make money when we become dependent. We are unknowingly allowing ourselves to be programmed.

We've all heard of the law of attraction. And it's a thing. But, there is also one of nature's laws that doesn't get as much publicity. This law is one that deals with opposites.

It is called the law of polarity. It brings balance. If there's an up, then there must be a down. If there is an inside to the room that you are in, then there is an outside to the room that you are in. This law of polarity decrees that you cannot be positive and negative minded at the same time. You are in control of this. So are you positive or negative? It's your choice. Choose wisely.

> *"How can there be too many children? That is like saying there are too many flowers."* — Mother Teresa

I am a public speaker. I speak on faith, attitude, and mindset. It's recession proof. I believe it, I love doing it, I'd like to think that I'm pretty good at it, and it's my calling. I've been asked to speak for all types of groups for different occasions over the years.

Do you know what my favorite type of event to speak at is? Can you keep a secret? Yeah? Okay, I'll tell you.

School assemblies.

What? Is he crazy? The germs!

Yeah, yeah. I know. But, you gotta understand where I'm coming from.

For starters, I love working with kids. There is no filter and they are so totally refreshing. There is no doubt if they like you, hate you, think that you're funny, think that you're boring, aren't sure about you, or whatever else it is that they are feeling. Their energy is authentic and contagious. If they're not feeling me, I need to work harder for them. It's as simple as that.

Next, I believe these kids—today's kids—have the opportunity to be the greatest generation that we've ever seen.

They have more awareness, and I find them to be more conscientious than generations before (despite what many think). Most of them aren't afraid to work hard (especially when they are inspired), and quite frankly, most of them haven't been punched in the face yet. They didn't go through the hardships and deal with everything that gets us jaded as we age. The sooner they can learn how magnificent they are, the better the chance they will have for success.

Finally, if you are someone who doesn't feel any of what I've just said, and you look at today's youth as a negative, just let me remind you of this: they'll be changing both of our diapers someday. Who do you think will get the extra diaper cream? Right. So, treat them well, teach them right, and let's move forward.

I go into these schools and speak at assemblies for the kids. Now, what I've found over the past few years is that what the administration wants me to focus on is vaping, juuling, drugs, drinking, suicide and bullying. I can touch on all of these subjects if need be. I prefer to do so quickly - very quickly - because I believe they are all important topics, but I don't like to give them too much energy.

Hold up. I just said they are important topics, right? Right. Then why move on quickly? Obviously, all of these are serious subjects. Although it's important to inform the kids about them, it's even more important to not have our youth obsess over them. I'm not into feeding energy to the negative. I'm about speaking life and hope into our youth.

I see. You don't agree. Well, let me give you a scenario.

Let's say I'm wanting to get into shape. Should I start eating from the local fast food dollar menu, get a lack of sleep and vape with my new favorite flavor? Or does it make more sense to get a solid, balance diet, get the rest that I need, and stay away from anything that will be harmful to my body?

What if I wanted to show you how to make a ridiculous amount of money? Should I direct you to start polling people that are in poverty, suggest that you pull out your debit card the second payday hits, and have you waste money on frivolous things that you don't need? Or, would you be better off for me to suggest that you study and associate with those who create wealth, have you invest with diversity, and create multiple income streams?

I'm thinking logic probably leans to option number two for both questions, right?

If that holds true (other than informing) why would it make sense for me to pull the kids attention in the direction of substance abuse, activities that will damage them physically and emotionally, and thoughts of things that would bring horrible consequences? Warning them is important, but I believe it would be better for me to advocate to these young minds to lift each other up, teach the benefits of getting healthy in mind, body and spirit, and how to create patterns of self-confidence and success. Sounds more appealing, right?

When I was a kid, I wasn't worried about what drugs would do to me, because they weren't anywhere in my realm. I was too busy trying to make gains in the weight room. Focus on what you want, not what you don't want.

> *"Whatever goal you give your subconscious mind, it will work night and day to achieve."* — Jack Canfield

You may have agreed with everything you've read so far, or I may have just blown your mind. I hope I didn't, because this next part is specifically about your mind. And, this part is VITAL.

The subconscious mind is something that I've spoken about at seminars. There are entire books written about it alone, but I'd like to save you a little time and give you some cheat codes and cliff notes.

You have your conscious mind (the decision-making part of your brain), and your subconscious mind (programs that are constantly running in the background). Your conscious mind runs the show, makes decisions and is the boss. The subconscious mind obeys. If you know how to control this, you can have a life of unlimited success. If you don't understand how this works, it can be dangerous for you and unknowingly create massive, consistent self-sabotage. Here's how this works.

Let's use the analogy that your brain is a ship. The conscious mind is the captain of the ship, and the subconscious mind is the crew. The captain directs the ship, gives orders, and will signal the crew. The crew doesn't make any decisions because it's not their job. The crew's job is only to obey the captain. The crew does not know where they are going; they follow orders. This crew (your subconscious mind) will steer the ship into the rocks if given inaccurate directions from the captain (your conscious mind) because the crew isn't here to debate, suggest or correct. The crew only follows orders.

The crew is incapable of understanding jokes, exaggerations, or indecisiveness. The crew does not talk back. The crew never stops working and this crew ALWAYS follows orders.

Just like the captain is the master of the ship, with all his orders being carried out, so to is the conscious mind the master of your mind, body, business and environment. And, just like the crew will obey the captain, your subconscious mind will obey the conscious mind. Your subconscious mind will take the orders it is fed and believe it as fact. If you were to tell yourself that you aren't qualified for that promotion, not good enough to make the team, or that you can't afford something, your powerful subconscious mind will follow those orders. You can expect your subconscious mind will work very hard on your behalf (following your orders) to not have you in the position to get that promotion, make that team or afford what you want.

Likewise, if the captain gives the right orders, there can be success and smooth sailing. If your belief is constant and strong, the crew, being your subconscious mind, will work very hard and the law of attraction will kick in creating success. Imagination of feeling and belief is powerful here - subconscious mind can't determine the difference. It obeys.

After only six months of being in the professional wrestling industry, I found myself on live, international television as a referee with the WWE. I debuted the exact same night as the first aired vignette of CM Punk. I envisioned it. I spoke it. Day and night I dreamed about it. And, it happened.

You don't need to understand *how* this works in order for it to do so, you just need to understand that it does. I don't understand how my dishwasher works, but it cleans the dishes when I press the power button. This is why vision boards can be so powerful. More on that when we speak about a different key in the upcoming chapter "Vision."

I know this may be shocking or a little heavy. It is critical for your own mindset and self being and success that you view yourself NOT AS IS, but as desired! Cast self-doubt and negativity away immediately and focus on what you WANT, not what you DON'T WANT. Stop gravitating to the impossibilities and start clinging to all of the unlimited possibilities. If you are going to climb higher you need to see where you will be and not continue to see yourself where you are. Your current situation is not your final destination.

## RANT #2

# RAW WARNING

*"Everybody pities the weak; jealousy you have to earn."* — Arnold Schwarzenegger

ONE OF THESE days you won't have a tomorrow. You don't live twice, you aren't guaranteed anything, and you don't get more time.

There is an old saying that says most people will tiptoe through life trying to make it safely to death. That ends right now. Worry and being indecisive is counterproductive. All it does is suck the life and energy out of you and your precious time. This is a time for you to stand up and be strong. Weak doesn't work.

Some people are inspired by motivational memes. Others are attracted to the speaker who raises their voice with emotion or gets shock value and curses just to curse. Some love the ones who can tell the story that will make you cry.

If you're looking for that, I'm about to disappoint you. None of that is me.

If I say something that you find inspiring, it isn't "rah-rah." You were inspired because it was authentic. I am passionate, but I don't yell to yell. I can promise that I'm never going to spit expletives to get your attention because I'm not an amateur, and if you cry - it wasn't my plan to make you. You simply felt my message that much. All I have to offer is 100% "real." I'm going to give that to you now.

This is the part where I go straight savage. I mean hungry lion busting out of the cage type of savage. And I may hurt some feelings here, but it's not because I'm trying to hurt feelings. It's because I'm going to say what you need to hear, not what you want to hear. Let's not waste each other's time.

This next part isn't a kick in the rear. It's a call to action. This is titled "Raw Warning" because it is raw and it's in your face. It's also a warning to end all nonsense, fake fear, or second guessing that may be holding you back. It's time to rise up and win, which won't get done by putting things off until tomorrow.

We are groomed to be soft. We are groomed to be distracted. We are groomed to be comfortable. It is easy to become complacent and lazy. But, you're better than that and it's time for you to start living your best life NOW.

Maybe you've been playing small. Maybe, just maybe you haven't been reaching your highest potential. Let's be honest. You have so much more to offer than what you've been giving. You may be sick of it too. It's time to stop holding back.

There are opportunities all around you begging for you, SCREAMING at you to simply go grab them.

Now, right here there is a fork in the road and there are only two ways that you can go. Either something just resonated, and you are serious about getting better and being the best you (You are my kind of people and we WILL make positive changes). Or, you just made a smirk, you knew better and put this book down so you could grab a latte, scroll your Twitter feed, and see who's on the mound for your team tonight. I guess some people have it all figured out. I also wonder how that's working for them. It's okay to not know everything all the time. We don't need more experts running around here. What we need is more people who are are secure enough, big enough, and real enough to say "You know what? I know what I know, but I don't have all the answers. I'm ready to learn. I'm ready to receive."

That's who I'm talking to in this book. I want to work with the master novice. The sponge. The one who wants to keep growing into their best self. That's who I want to run with.

*Just to be clear, I don't have all the answers either. Nobody does. If any of these "experts" tell you that they do, they're either wrong or straight up lying. Run. Fast. I'm simply sharing ideas, and extending my hand to help lift others up. We need more of that.*

The bottom line is this - you and I live like royalty. This shouldn't cause entitlement, because entitled is unattractive and spoiled. Entitlement is ugly.

Some don't see that they live like royalty and feel like a victim. Life's not fair. It It never was. It's not now and it probably never will be. Everyone has their own problems, but you shouldn't have a victim mentality. YOU ARE NOT A VICTIM!!!

What we should embrace is gratitude for who and where we are right now. The journey is still happening, but we need to be thankful. Why?

Take a minute and think what it would be like if you had your place in life traded. That's right. Go trade it with the kid in that third-world country who has the wrong winner on his World Series' t-shirt that he got as a "gift" so some corporation gains a tax write-off. You know, the kid who smiles for the camera even though he knows he's gonna maybe eat once today, kick a half deflated soccer ball on a dirt "field", and go to bed tonight laying on the world's worst mattress which has bugs and smells like piss. That kid is out there. You have a roof. And a bed. And wifi. Have you woken up? Good. We needed a shakeup.

Let's make a conscious decision to be a solution to somebody today, not a problem. Everybody you interact with today is fighting a BATTLE that you (praise God) couldn't understand and have no clue about! Be thankful, and don't talk about what you can't do, explore what you can do.

You know how you have that thing that hurts? You know, that tooth that's been bothering you, or maybe your back? I'm sure those things that are bothering you are real, but do you know what's really going to hurt? Regret.

Before you become the one at the end of their life with no more time and tons of that ugly regret, I'm suggesting that you take an attitude of offense. There is no time for any weak mindset or holding back. When you do hold back, we miss out on the gift of you. Make it better. Make it right.

You get better. You get right. Be a beacon. Don't be selfish. We need more givers and less takers. Give!

Get that thing done today. You may not get another today. This is your reminder - your warning. You have only so many sleeps, breaths and days left. Going forward let's be on purpose and make every single one of them count.

I believe in forgiveness. I believe in second chances. I believe in you.

All your setback did was pave the way for your comeback. It's time, and we have work to do. You are about to grow and it's going to make other people uncomfortable. Grow anyway.

I'm glad you're still here. Let's make the most of it.

# KEY 2

# ATTITUDE
# (LOSE THE LOSER)

*"Everybody has the appetite for success, but most don't have the stomach for it."* — Former NFL Player & Author James Williams

**I BELIEVE THERE** is a misconception about being positive. Positivity doesn't mean being simple and foolish with rose colored glasses where everything is great regardless of circumstances because I'm eating glitter cupcakes on my unicorn. Positivity is powerful. Being positive means that you look for the best, expect the best, and are mentally strong enough to guard your mind from toxicity.

If you consider yourself as someone in the negative camp, you're killing me. You're actually killing yourself, too. Like, really.

The negativity has to stop. I don't mean basic trashing someone, or pulling other people down, bully-style negativity. We need to cease and desist with that too, but here I'm directly speaking of the "defeatist mentality" you may not even realize you have. This is an underlying programmed type of negativity.

All day long I run into people who have it. They'll explain what can't, shouldn't, and won't be done instead of what can, should, and will. There are hardly any declarations of achievement anymore. Everybody just settles.

What's unsettling is to see how many people are wired wrong. Wired in the sense of leaning toward the negative versus the positive. This appears to be a vicious cycle, because it's been here throughout history. It's like an incurable infection that gets handed down from generation to generation. And this negativity is dangerous because no one is immune. It does not discriminate against age, race, religious belief, location, or profession. I see it across the board. Just as an example, the following little adventures that I'm about to share with you were incidents that I have experienced and witnessed where this infection spread in a literal single calendar week.

> *"Show me a good loser, and I'll show you a loser."* — Vince Lombardi

I'll refrain from naming the specific team or even the sport, but I remember being very frustrated with the overall tone from this single, distinct example of when a negative attitude was the root of unnecessary failure. During this one season in particular, "Team A" (as we will call them) was a very good, well known, solid high school squad with potential to go very, very far that year. As they moved through the brackets, they mauled the teams they were supposed to beat, and in winning fashion mustered and found a way to win against other really good teams, as potential champions should.

There was one problem. They had it. They were infected. For some unexplained reason, the belief meter was at zero. I personally couldn't understand it. I mean, the skill was there. They had nationally ranked kids, rising stars, and even a state champion senior on the team. On paper this was a dangerous squad that had maximum potential.

But I guess that's it, huh? That word "potential?" Potential is great, but it can be misleading. The actual definition of the word potential is "having or showing the capacity to become or develop into something in the future." Let me translate. Potential means "you haven't done anything yet." Dag. And if there is no belief, well that potential is rendered useless. Damaged goods. Send it back. Wasted potential.

Like I mentioned, Team A had tons of it (potential), but had no vision for themselves. On the few occasions where they had to match up against a superior ranked team, they didn't have belief, and they wasted that potential. They believed what was on paper, and they predicted the outcome in their minds before even entering the contest.

I heard, "We're gonna get killed." I'm not surprised at much anymore these days, but that one just left me shaking my head. You couldn't talk to them either. That negative wiring was in full force.

"Are you kidding?" I heard. "They have this guy, and that guy. And, THAT kid is a state champion."

I heard it from some of the parents, too.

"Oh, we have a good team but this other team is really good."

Seriously people? Oh ye of such little faith. The way I saw it was that *we* have this guy, and that guy, and OUR kid is a state champion. But, I was in the minority.

The results were predictable. Team A—that very good, well known, solid high school squad with potential to go very, very far that year—got slaughtered. Embarrassed. Team A players were actually laughing during the massacre. I've coached for years, and that's when you know it's bad. When it's so bad that you are beyond being upset because it's so far out of hand? Yeah. That's really bad.

It was so avoidable, too. Because of that half-empty mindset I was personally annoyed that I wasted gas money and the two hours of my life that I'll never get back, because all in all, that loss didn't need to be a loss. I had hope for them, but I should have known better because they actually told me (and themselves) what was going to happen.

The players believed what they READ on paper versus believing in THEMSELVES.

Henry Ford said "Whether you think you can, or you can't—you're right." That day, Team A was right. They deemed themselves losers, and they lost.

> *"I've never responded well to entrenched negative thinking."* — David Bowie

I was standing in a Wawa. What? What's a "Wawa?" I don't believe you just questioned that. I'm watching you.

Think convenience store—with gas pumps. And breakfast bowls. And footlong sandwiches. And smoothies. Mmmmmm…smoothies…

Anyway, Wawa was bumpin'. The place was packed with everyone trying to get somewhere. I was standing in line. Maybe I had a smoothie. Maybe I had a shortie. It doesn't matter.

What mattered was that there was this guy in front of me. And there was a guy behind me too. The guy in front of me apparently knew and was speaking to the guy behind me. Over me. Got the picture? I was the cream and they were the cookies in the Oreo of a conversation that I didn't want to be in. I was the annoying person doing nothing wrong that happened to be in their way because they decided to talk to one another. It was a little obnoxious, fairly uncomfortable, and they had it. Both of them. They were infected with the bad wiring. And, it was driving me nuts.

"Hey Joe—how's the wife?" The first man shouted over me (as if I wasn't standing there).

"Ah, she's alright. You know," 'Joe' shouted back.

"How you doin'?" (No. Really. He asked that.)

"I'm alright. I could be better. I'm still breathing."

Yuck. I cringed.

"Hey," the first guy yells. "We're still surviving. That's all you can ask for. That's all we can do."

"Yeah, you can't win 'em all."

Wait. What? Bro, I can't take it. Let me get my four dollar sandwich and peace out.

I don't even know what they said except negative, negative, negative. La, la, la, la. Negative. By the way they were speaking you would think someone just kidnapped their puppy or something. That whole situation was even worse than you not knowing what a Wawa is. I can't even stand it.

I mean these guys were in a community, fully clothed. Buying food. With money. In air conditioning. They were about to leave with freedom under their own power and get into vehicles that they owned and drive away to go wherever they chose. They were living like kings and they didn't even know it. But the infected, bad attitude—that bad wiring got 'em.

See, here's the problem. That's not "all you can ask for," and that's not "all we can do." We are not put here only to "survive." We are put here to thrive! Do you understand what can happen when you unleash your mind? Do you realize the possibilities of what can happen when you take this self created limitation off of yourself? Do you understand the type of energy you create when you give yourself permission to succeed? Do you even know how?? Read on and let's start to realize and accept how great we really are and can be.

> *"Money can't buy you happiness, but it can buy you a yacht big enough to pull up right alongside it."* — David Lee Roth

A few years ago, an experiment was run in a very popular tristate publication's classified section. Two identical adds were posted side by side with the same exact job description and requirements. They had the same location, same field, same necessary qualifications, same everything. The only difference was that one employment opportunity had the annual salary listed as one hundred twenty thousand dollars a year. The other listing suggested fifty percent less annual income boasting and posting at sixty thousand dollars per year.

An overwhelming eighty percent plus of applicants (I'll say that again), eighty percent plus of applicants applied for the sixty thousand dollar job. Not to be redundant, but again, both jobs had the exact same description and requirements while one position offered double the pay. Eighty percent applied for the lower paying job. This puts a glaring spotlight on confidence and self worth. I'm sorry… does that bother anyone else? Just me? Okay…

Most people played low, stayed in their lane, didn't "go for it." Yuck. Was it too good to be true? Was there a catch? Must have been. Maybe, just maybe, all those people conveniently missed the better opportunity. Or, maybe not. Maybe this says a ton about how we decide to play not to lose instead of making the unwavering decision of playing to win.

> *"More the knowledge lesser the Ego, lesser the knowledge, more the Ego."* — Albert Einstein

Attitude is imperative to success. How you see yourself is critical. But, could there be such a thing that we dare imply where there could be "too much" attitude? Of course there is. You recognize it as ego.

Every DJ I talk to is the absolute greatest freakin' thing since Grandmaster Flash. Just ask them, usually they'll tell you. They pack the dance floors, book gigs by accident and have crowds of people adoring them. Or not. There is an interesting comparison to see who has what equipment (What software do you use?), the big venue they last booked, who they know, and blah, blah, blah.

How about corporate America? "Do you know who I am?" "Do you know who you are talking to?" "Oh, you must not have heard." "Who's your VP?" It's like an uncontrollable, fast spreading disease in American business. There's too many important people. If this hurts to read right now, maybe it's because you know I'm talking about you. I'm not saying you're not important. I'm saying not everybody needs to be told how important you really are. They can figure it out on their own.

It's with actors, coaches, parents at the school functions, business executives, the musician, professors, on and on and on. We see that ugly ego rear it's head in almost every arena of life.

When I was in professional wrestling, ego and self pride was rampant. Especially on the independent scene, or in the "indies." What I did notice was the bigger the star, or if it was a ring veteran who had many years in the business, the less self-pride. They realized they didn't need to prove themselves. That's the interesting part. It seems the more secure someone is, the less the feel for the need to boast.

In 1985, the number one song "We Are The World" was recorded by 46 singers in a supergroup named "USA For Africa." The recording sold over ten million copies worldwide, where proceeds resulted in charity intended for aid to Africa.

Some of the biggest musical artists of all time were a part of this recording. This isn't an exaggeration. I mean the absolute biggest names in the world were a part of this lineup. Michael Jackson, Bruce Springsteen, Billy Joel, Stevie

Wonder, Bob Dylan, and Cyndi Lauper were only just a few who were a part of this historical moment.

Musical icon Quincy Jones was the producer of this monstrosity. Rumors and legend of the recording sessions became fact that Quincy posted a handwritten sign that read "Check your egos at the door."

Could you imagine?

"Hi. I'm Michael Jackson. I'd shake your hand, but I'm wearing my glove."

"Well, hello Michael. I'm the guy with two first names. Billy Joel. But you can call me the 'Piano Man.'"

"Oh hi-ya, boys! I'm Cyndi Lauper. Excuse me while Tina Turner and I run to the ladies room because ya' know, girls just wanna have fun."

Breh.

It is ridiculous to even try and picture this, right? How could you possibly have all of those megastars coexist together in one studio? In a world where simple four or five piece bands can't stay together because of personality clashes, this was setup to be one pompous, vanity, swagger filled pride fest.

The story goes that other than some creative differences, this project was what it was intended to be. According to Quincy Jones, "You had 46 of the biggest recording stars in the entire world in one room who were totally committed to what we were trying to achieve… to help people in a far-off place who were in desperate need."

I guess Lionel Ritchie didn't have to explain to Willie Nelson who he was. They all were different, all recognized they were all great for their own contributions, and it sounds as if they all had enough self confidence that ego wasn't on the radar. Tremendous.

You should love yourself. You should be confident. Attitude is critical, but crossing the line into conceit is dangerous. Ego gets you hurt.

> *"My momma told me, you better shop around."* — Smokey Robinson

There I was in the "Keystone State" of Pennsylvania shopping around my first released book *"Get Up (Encouraging You To Attack Life)."* It was early 2018, and although *"Get Up"* already went to the top of the Self Help category in Amazon, in my mind that wasn't good enough. Obviously, I believe in the message, so I was in the process of trying to get as many eyes and ears on it that I could. One day I was stopping at bookstores when I popped into what was once a fairly known larger retailer in my County.

The girl behind the counter looked to be in her late teens with glasses that seemed to be too big for her head, but were somehow kept on by her cropped, blue hair. I don't have glasses, or hair, so I was intrigued.

She started to explain to me that they lost their lease and the store was unfortunately shutting down in the next month, so the chance of me having a book signing there would be an "impossibility."

Sigh. There's that brainwave again. I saw 30 days. I saw me marketing like a beast for the next seven days and packing their place on the eighth. I saw a last "hurrah" with their store going out with a bang. All I saw were possibilities. All she gave me was an "impossibility," but I was told when the manager came back in I could see if he had any suggestions.

Emerging from his smoke break, this melancholy, stoic, tall, slender man slid behind his desktop monitor at the counter. I was rightfully assuming that this was the manager. As he settled in, my "impossible" millennial began describing to him why I was there. As she was explaining things to him I couldn't help but notice something. The entire time from when she started speaking until when she ended with asking if he had any suggestions for me, he continually shook his head "No."

No? No what? No why? Just "No?"

This guy. Low energy. This whole scenario was wired wrong.

Still without ever looking at or facing me, for the first time in the conversation I was acknowledged. "Melancholy Man" let out a sigh of defeat. He paused, then gave his head another wag of "No," and actually referred me back to the first book store I went to in my own backyard who initially denied me.

And then he murmured, "That's your only hope."

My only hope? My only hope? Seriously??

Okay. You know what people? Hold my book while I run into traffic. I needed a mental detox after that one. My only hope. If that truly was "my only hope," I would be hopeless.

I politely thanked them for their time, quickly exited the store and proceeded to the next establishment where I met the owner and right then and there nailed a date for another book signing. Don't buy into the limitations that other people have in mind for you. Create your own circumstances by getting rid of the defeatist, loser mindset.

> *"And let that be a lesson to you all. Nobody beats Vitas Gerulaitis 17 times in a row."* — Vitas Gerulaitis after defeating Jimmy Connors at the January 1980 Masters in tennis after losing the previous 16 matches.

Do you want to win? Do you want to be a beast at your craft? Seriously. Do you want to be a force? Do you want to be known as the one that people are talking about no matter what your place in life is? Then you need to fall in love with this next idea.

You need to have a refuse to lose attitude. It needs to be no matter what. You cannot accept the idea of giving up. Hold on. I know that can be a lot to internalize. Let me put it another way. Let me speak in negatives as far as what we are not to do.

We need to not have "impossibilities." We need to visualize and create possibilities.

We need to not think that one option is our "only hope." We need to visualize, create and become hope.

We need to not believe that "That's all you can ask for and all you can do is survive." We need to learn that this is a lie. We were not meant to simply survive. We were put here to flourish.

We need to not have the mindset that you are going to get "killed." We need to start believing that you are going to crush it.

Not buying it? Well, you should. And, you should you buy a lot of it. The ones who win have major stock in what I'm saying here.

Start by turning off the news. There's nothing uplifting on it anyway. Turn off the radio. You've heard it all before and you're not missing out on anything great that is new. Netflix can chill. Put down the phone. News changes yet somehow stays the same, songs get old, and that phone will keep you hypnotized and paralyzed if you don't use it in increments and control it.

Listen, invest in yourself. If you're entertainment expense is higher than your education expense, you're cruising down the wrong road. Dive into some personal growth. Start reading and listening to things that will benefit your mind and spirit. Do it for a few minutes—maybe fifteen, each day. That will give you twenty three hours and forty five minutes to do anything and everything else you need to do. It will become infectious. You will start to look forward to it. You will start to change.

Now here comes the important part.

You have complete control over you and more times than not, the outcome of the circumstances. Everything you put in your mind, every word you specifically say, every thought you specifically think, and all the actions that you do is what makes it all happen. You are the equivalent of a choose your own adventure book.

Most people will not see this because they are victims. They are dictated to and succumb to situations. They accept. They accept too easily. They accept to lose.

Fall in love with the "last man standing" attitude. Refuse to go away. Choose to be positive. As soon as that negativity creeps in, cast it away. Understand that your mind is more powerful than the subconscious negativity, and consciously decide to make a habit of pushing it away. Do not accept. Demand. You are worthy, and you are worth it.

Lose the loser mindset. This isn't feel good talk. This is science. Any quantum physicist will agree. You can literally attract success into your life starting with gratitude and an attitude of positivity. Your thoughts create energy and energy is powerful!

Show your inner loser the door. It doesn't serve you. You need to either learn, relearn or remember the idea that you can win. Constantly. Let's get started. Keep reading on. We have galaxies to conquer.

## RANT #3

# DAYDREAM BREAKTHROUGH

*"If you can dream, you can do it. Always remember that this whole thing was started by a mouse."* — Walt Disney

**DO YOU WANT** to breakthrough? Of course you do. Everybody wants to level up. So why do so many just...not?

Hustle. Grind. Discipline. Attitude. Tenacity. Work ethic. Motivation. Beneficial habits. Every single one of these are key factors and attributes that are all important building blocks in your wall of success. But, if you truly want to reach your breakthrough, there is one all important exercise that you need to do on the daily.

What leaves me scratching my head is the fact that this practice is so looked down upon by most. It's made fun of. It's ridiculed at best and it's definitely discouraged in schools. If you do this next thing that I'm going to suggest, you will be viewed as someone who cannot concentrate, has no focus, and zero mental discipline. The truth of the matter is that if you can do this next technique, it's the total opposite as you do have tremendous focus, discipline, and concentration.

This is the foundation for success. And this isn't just me making things up in my imagination so I have something to write about. This is insinuated and mentioned in some of the most influential books from over the past one hundred and twenty years such as *"The Secret," "Power Of The Subconscious Mind," "Think And Grow Rich,"* and *"The Science Of Getting Rich"* just to name a few.

You need to daydream.

Remember back to when you were young, before life got in the way. Remember how you were fascinated with whatever that thing was? Maybe you pictured yourself on a stage with people cheering for you. Maybe you imagined yourself making a winning play for your team. Maybe you fantasized about living somewhere far away. Maybe you dreamed about what it would be like to be on a boat. Maybe you imagined that you would be the boss.

What happened? Did the world grow cold? Did life get hard? Did you grow up?

I want to encourage you to dream again. I want you to visualize your life, then live your vision. You were made for more, but you need to see that for yourself, because no one else can do it for you. There is way more waiting for you out there than just growing up, paying bills, getting old, and then someday dying. But you have to tune into that frequency.

You can't be what you can't see. See yourself on that stage. Get on that boat in your mind. Dream of being that leader who everyone values, respects, and listens to.

And, (here's the really important part) you need to feel it.

I mean really feel that moment. Hear the applause. What does it sound like? Put yourself there. What are you wearing? Are you moving? Are you smiling? Can you see the faces on the others? Are you warm? What does it feel like?

Dreaming and seeing yourself as is, is a key factor to breaking through. If you can dream it, you can be it. If you can believe it, you can be it. If you can see it, YOU CAN BE IT!

Hustle, grind, discipline, attitude, tenacity, work ethic, motivation, and beneficial habits are all very important spark plugs in your engine. But, dreaming that dream is the engine.

Put your head in the clouds. Gaze at those stars. Dream that dream. Remove all of those fictitious limits and start daydreaming again so you can see it, feel it, and then eventually BE it.

If you are going to be successful you need to see yourself as where you will be and not where you are. Do not let your present circumstances squash your future opportunities. The next upcoming key will be really powerful for you. Let's turn the page so we can really get into the crucial topic of vision.

## KEY 3

# VISION (SEE IT TO BE IT)

*"A man is what he thinks all day long."*
— Ralph Waldo Emerson

**BEFORE WE GET** started with this chapter, remember this rule from the "Daydream Breakthrough" rant: You can't be what you can't see.

When I say vision, I'm not referring about what you do with your eyes or some otherworldly superpower. Then what am I talking about? Now just hold on a minute. I'll ask the questions.

So, let me ask you this next question. It's simple, it's straightforward, and for most people it's probably one of the toughest ones to answer honestly.

How do you see yourself?

I ask that, because what you need to understand is that how you see yourself is crucial to your success. We can do the "motivation vs discipline vs skill" debate all day long but without vision you can only go so far.

Most of us operate by our five basic senses as in what we can see, hear, smell, taste, and touch. We at the Hayford home have three dogs: Molly, Pablo and Tinkerbell. They can all hear, see, smell, taste and touch. That just means, you and Tinkerbell are on the same level when it comes to the outside world.

But that inside world is different.

Unfortunately for Molly, Pablo, Tinkerbell, our old turtle Gertie, and my favorite chicken Sweet Mae Brown, they don't have what you and I are blessed with as humans. You were born with higher faculties such as imagination, intuition, perception, will, and reason. I think most of the time we take this for granted and don't appreciate or utilize these amazing gifts for what they truly are. We stay locked in this physical, outside world even though we can make such massive strides with our lives if we start paying attention to and taking advantage of these other benefits that we are in possession of.

Here's another question for you (I have a ton of them).

What do you want?

I didn't ask "What do you want and how you are going to get it?" Don't worry about the "how" just yet. I simply asked you "What do you want?" Do you know what you want? Do you have a dream? Do you have a goal? Do you have vision?

Bob Proctor is an author, public speaker, and one of today's leading advocates for this theory. You may know him best for his work from the 2007 movie "*The Secret.*" Years ago Bob was featured on a program where he was being interviewed. During the show he ran with the conversation, changed the pace and even started to question the interviewer.

He said "The first thing you do is sit down and decide what you want. If it's money, it's how much money…"

The interviewer attempting to be witty immediately blurted out "Lots of."

Bob responded even quicker than the interruption itself with a confident reply of "Well, nobody knows how much 'lots of' is. So you've got be specific."

The announcer replied with a retreating "OK."

You have to be on purpose and - here's the key - specific with your vision.

When you are in prayer, pray specifically.

When you are asking for something, ask specifically.

When you think about that thing that keeps you up at night with excitement, think specifically.

When you picture yourself as that person you are aspiring to be, picture yourself specifically.

When you have that thing that you are daydreaming or imagining about, daydream and imagine specifically.

When you desire, desire specifically.

And all those things just mentioned need to happen. Pray, ask, think, picture, daydream, imagine and desire need to be part of what you are doing as you are chasing your dream because this will create that ever so important VISION.

I can't stress this enough. You wouldn't text a friend with a bunch of mixed, random letters from the alphabet. It wouldn't make sense and it wouldn't be definitive. This is the exact same principle for your vision. Be so specific that what you want is crystal clear in your mind. You need to be able to picture it clear as day down to how it feels, where you are and even what you are wearing.

*"We become what we think about."* — Earl Nightingale

Earl Nightingale also said something to the affect of "If most people were thinking out loud, they'd be speechless." But, he said zillions of great things so let's just move forward.

Whether we realize it or not, understand it or not, or even like it or not, the fact of the matter is that we have all been programmed. From before some of our earliest memories when they first started to become created until now, we have been thinking in a paradigm, or methodology that for most of us has been shaped by others. We still unknowingly get programmed today. The marketing, music, messages, slogans, news, etc, all continually rewire out brain with patterns that we constantly get exposed to.

The repetition of sustained, consecutive thoughts create power. That power can be beneficial or detrimental. So, here comes another question for you.

What are you telling yourself?

I ask because what you are telling yourself each day will either lift you up or drag you down. Here's the good news. You are in control of what you are focusing on. You are also in control of what you are giving your time, energy, and attention to, and ultimately accepting. Feed your mind and focus on the positive. If you want faster results with this, feed your mind and focus on the positive repetitively and more often.

Besides those repetitive, beneficial thoughts that you are thinking, visualize your success with the same repetition. This visualization needs to be specific.

Kevin Na is a golfer for the PGA. Memorial Day Weekend of 2019 he played in the "Charles Schwab Challenge" at the Colonial Country Club located in Fort Worth Texas. Na has had other PGA victories before, but he never captured one at the Colonial.

Coming to the end of a relaxed family weekend, my wife and I wound it down by watching the end of this event. Christina is an avid golfer herself, and this one was fun to take in as a fan. It was very competitive and jam packed with some of the top names of the day.

When it was all said and done, it was dramatic, it was decisive, and for the first time in his career, Kevin Na won at the Colonial. His name is now forever attached to some of the greatest to ever play the game who have won at the Colonial like Arnold Palmer, Jack Nicklaus, and Ben Hogan.

So, good for him. You don't care about golf. Those names mean nothing to you. Big deal. Get to it. What did he win?

Okay. Besides the respect and accolades for all his hard work, he pocketed approximately 1.3 million dollars. And you said golf is lame.

He celebrated with his pregnant wife and media magnet daughter, Sophia. There were smiles, cheers, and hugs. Not only did he win the money, respect, and accolades, he also won the vintage, mint condition 1973 Dodge Challenger muscle car. What did he do next? He immediately gave it to his long time friend and caddie, Kenny. I'm not crying. You're crying.

As it was getting late and the hoopla started dying down, Christina deserted me for the comfort of our bedroom. I stayed put on the couch with the golf network on and started drifting off, until out of nowhere something caught my attention.

Na (while holding Sophia - pass me a Kleenex, please) was interviewed. The interviewer proclaimed that next time Mr. Na returned to that course, he will get to see his name on the Colonial "Wall Of Champions." He was asked how that made him feel.

His response was glazed over by most, but it woke me up and gave me chills. I rewound it, recorded it, and watched it back at least fifty times.

He said "It feels great. Standing on the first tee, I looked at that wall, and IN MY HEAD I ENGRAVED MY NAME IN IT. And, sure enough, it's gonna be there."

That's what he told us, but I'm sure imagining - or engraving - his name on the Wall Of Champions didn't happen for the first time as he was about to step into the tee box. I'm sure that was the last time he imagined that, before actually going out and making it happen.

I'll state it again. Visualization needs to be specific.

That's why they call vision boards, vision boards. They are supposed to create vision. Just like the one my wife Christina has placed next to her side of our bed did.

It is placed there purposely. She looks at it each night and makes sure it is the last thing that she sees before going to sleep, while being the first thing that she sees when she wakes up. It is has various visuals that are geared for all her goals and dreams, both long and short term.

I noticed that there was a section that had pictures of palm trees, people relaxing on a beach, and a picture where it was "only" Christina, our daughter Jayda, and "Grandma Lee." I say only because it doesn't have me, neither of our sons, and definitely not our dogs Molly, Pablo or Tinkerbell. What's up wit' dat?

January 2019 comes around and so does an opportunity to go to Hawaii. Hold on. I didn't say a shopping spree at Walmart. I said an opportunity to go to Hawaii.

My older son Kane was wrestling varsity for his high school with an aggressive schedule, while my younger son Harrison was pinning and winning for his eight grade middle school team. Too many matches, too many meets, and wanting to give the illusion that I am actually a responsible parent, I urged my wife to "go with the girls." As you could imagine, she happily obliged.

About the third night after they left (yes, first Christina left me on the couch falling asleep to Kevin Na and then she left me in freezing Pennsylvania) I was laying in bed and realized that her vision happened. I don't believe that she actually meant to have a goal of going with her mom and J exclusively to Hawaii, but it's what she looked at every single night and every single day for months while letting it burn into her subconscious. Coincidence? I don't believe in them.

All I know is, they were walking on beaches in Maui, and I was shoveling snow near Philly. Focus on what you want, not what you don't want.

*"I dream my painting then I paint my dream."* — Vincent van Gogh

Do you like the Police? No, I don't mean the guy who pulls you over for speeding. I'm talking about about the rock group. You know, Sting? Well of course you do!

In September of 2013 Sting was a featured guest on the Dave Letterman Show. For whatever reason the conversation didn't start off about new music, latest projects, or something to promote. Letterman asked Sting (or Gordon Sumner to you) about his childhood. His childhood? Seriously? Like, really.

I found it interesting that many in the audience and Lettermen himself found humor in much of what Sting was saying, when I found it to be fascinating and powerful. Sometimes I just hear things differently, or play on a different frequency. I still haven't figured out if this is a good or bad thing.

He explained about his upbringing in a small ship town in England where one of his earliest memories is of "the sky being blotted out by a massive ship towering above the house."

Super tankers, liners and warships were everyday life where his grandfather and father worked in the shipyard right at the end of his street. As Letterman seemed (in my opinion) to glaze right past the magnitude of this next statement, Sting described that as a young boy he would "Watch the men go to work every morning and think 'Is that my destiny?' "

"Right," Letterman said without blinking and racing to the next question. I on the other hand felt the power in what that young boy was thinking. All he saw was all he saw. If he wasn't going to be a dockworker, shipmate, or whatever, that little boy without YouTube or a smartphone needed vision.

He went on to note that one time in particular there was a motorcade driving through town (possibly to christen a ship) and it was the Royal Family. He remembers being a young boy standing in the street with his Mom, watching the cars slowly roll by, all while waving his little, British flag. Inside one particular slow moving Rolls Royce was the Queen Mother who took notice of the patriotic little boy and waved to him. He waved back and she gave a warm smile. Then he had a thought.

"I don't really want to be in the street. I don't want to be in that shipyard. I want to be in that car."

The crowd roared with laughter. I lost my breath. Sting wiped his eye.

Letterman seeming to feel the flow of the interview then asked "Was that the moment you knew there was a life bigger than what you've experienced?"

The Police frontman answered honestly. "I had no idea how to get that life, but I knew I wanted comfort. I wanted security. I wanted privilege. I wanted money."

The crowd murmured as he shrugged his shoulders as if he did something wrong in their eyes and said "Just being honest."

Keeping vision and a desire of wanting something more, it finally happened when his uncle left behind a four stringed guitar. Sting claimed that as soon as he saw that guitar he knew he found his "route out" and "best friend" as he didn't speak for four years and just played.

Wrapping the segment he spoke of the Beatles coming to his realm of awareness. Sting said "They conquered the world and they gave permission to a whole generation of kids 'like me' a chance to try ourselves. And, I owe them a lot."

Small talk, one liners, and everything commercialized continued, but that one got me. The imagination, the intuition, and the vision that he described in a four minute interview that was meant to be light and entertaining gave me goosebumps.

See past your circumstances. See past your Goliath. Know that your current situation is not your final destination and create that vision. If a little boy in a cold, English shipyard without wifi can do it, so can you.

> *"Doctors and scientists said breaking the four-minute mile was impossible, that one would die in the attempt. Thus, when I got up from the track after collapsing at the finish line, I figured I was dead."* — Sports Illustrated first ever "Sportsman Of The Year" Sir Roger Bannister

The bigger and scarier the goal, the more people laughing at you, along with all the people giving you rational reasons as to why you're nuts because whatever you are doing is "impossible" means that you're onto something. You are striving for things that others can't, haven't or wouldn't attempt to achieve. Most people only believe what they see.

The timing of the track and field event of the mile was first recorded back in 1850 - before the Civil War!

Roger Bannister is the first human being in history to run a mile in under 4 minutes. But, "so what" because records are made to be broken, right? Well, this one is different. Not only was it never done before, but it was impossible. Physically, humanly impossible. At least that's what the "experts" claimed.

Experts also claimed that the human heart could explode. The lung capacity could not physically endure the tension and bodies simply were not made to perform like this.

In 1945 the stunning, unattainable record of 4:01 was set. Amazing! And, what a record it was - as it stood for close to the next decade. But in 1954 Roger Bannister didn't listen to critics, experts or anyone else. The man who once said "It is the brain, not the heart or lungs, that is the critical organ" crossed the finish line to a thundering ovation and a new world record with a final time of 3 minutes and 59.4 seconds.

But that's not the incredible part. The real head scratcher here lies within the fact that something once deemed so physically impossible - this unimaginable record which once previously lasted close to a decade - now only stood for a month and a half! As a matter of fact by 1957 (just 3 years from when Bannister originally broke the record) FIFTEEN runners also surpassed the 4 minute mile. Today the 4 minute mile is pretty common and is considered pedestrian among runners while at one point, science and medicine's most educated and trained authorities in human anatomy claimed this to be totally inconceivable.

This story has so much more to it than just setting a world record, or even being about what the body can do when the mind makes a decision. This story is all about casting vision for others. Once Bannister achieved success, it showed others what was possible and limitations were lifted off of minds all because of vision.

Blocks and restrictions exist only in our minds. We need to see past those limitations. The masses? They have it all wrong. Most believe it when they see it. The trick is to believe it, and *then* you'll see it.

## RANT #4

# REPETITION

*"Success isn't always about 'Greatness', it's about consistency. Consistent, hard work gains success. Greatness will come."* — Dwayne "The Rock" Johnson

**REMEMBER GUNS 'N** Roses? Well of course you do, Sunshine! "Welcome To The Jungle," "Sweet Child O' Mine," and "Paradise City" are just a few of the top hits that may ring a bell.

"Duff" or Duff McKagan (as named by his parents) from the iconic late 80s/early 90s rock group spoke to the band's success when he appeared on the *"Rich Eisen Show"* in the spring of 2019.

Duff suggested that the success of G 'N' R and other musical acts that sprouted with roots from Seattle—ya know—the "Grunge Era," I'm assuming? Nirvana, Pearl Jam, Soundgarden, Alice In Chains, Mudhoney, on and on, was fostered because: "I attribute the talent to…one thing.

It rains a lot there...so everybody goes to their garage and basement and plays."

What? It rained. That's it? Did he just say that Guns 'N freaking Roses were successful because of the weather? Pretty much.

My interpretation? Repetition.

It's all repetition. You want to run that marathon? Run repetitively. You want to sing that song? Sing repetitively. Kick that goal in soccer? Kick repetitively. Nail that speech? Speak it repetitively. Rewire that brain. Train it. Retrain it. Learn.

Over and over and over and over again wins. Do you go to the gym once, bust out some sit ups and crunches and think "Yeah, baby. Abs for life! Check the washboard." Of course not. Your consistency is what creates your results.

Duff spoke about retreating to garages and basements. Let me ask you something. What's your garage? Is it the baseball diamond? Is it your network marketing biz that you refer to as your side hustle? Is it growing your social media? Is it your portfolio or investments that you make? Is it that ever annoying, elusive goal?

Here's some good news. You don't need it to rain. Sunshine doesn't have to go away to convince you that there is nothing else to do but work on your craft. You gotta roll up them sleeves, bring your lunch pail, and get ready to work it. If you don't put in the work, what do you actually expect? Success? Without work? Are you just magically going to somehow become accidentally successful?

Ouch. That sucked.

But it's straight fire, and you know it's true. You don't need to be told what to do, you just need to go and do it.

And you need to do it over and over and over and over and over again until your brain is so rewired that it just comes natural to you.

Success is so not what people want you to believe it is. Success is ugly, mundane, never-ending work that creates a lifestyle and a legacy that can be enjoyed forever. Want to challenge that statement? Bad move. Come at me, bro. I'm from Jersey. Jersey!

Actually, forget about me. This is about you. If you're skeptical about this message, go do your own homework. Check any recognizable, current household name, to the game changers throughout history from ancient times and days of yore, to present champions and trendsetters. Success ain't purdy. No, sir. Success be a down right dogfight. If you choose to pursue success and believe different, you are setting yourself up for a big, fat fail.

Let's end this debate (as if there ever was one in the first place) once and for all. Do you know how ballet is so elegant, flawless and beautiful? The ballerinas that perform it are living art, and somehow seem to flow like water. They are majestic and represent beauty and tranquility with an expression of grace.

Now...back to you for a quick sec. Your phone? Yes, I know. It's right next to you. And, no. I'm not a creeper, I don't have special powers, and I am not a psychic. But I've learned that we learn habits. Your phone is your habit. Let's take this rare moment and use it for something productive. Okay?

Pick it up.

Do us a favor and google "what success looks like ballerinas."

I'll wait.

Seriously. Stop reading. Pick up your phone and just google "what success looks like ballerinas." Now go to images.

OMG. You think this is being bossy? Just wait until you hear how I yell at you when this audio book comes out. I'll be yelling with love, of course. And the audiobook will be produced by THE Carl Bahner. I digress.

"What success looks like ballerinas" is mesmerizing and yet somehow hard to look at in the same instance, right? Yikes. The busted up, beaten toes, bruised, bloodied and bandaid wrapped feet represent something. They represent all that work that created success.

Success came from over and over and over and over again. In other words, success came from...

Repetition.

There's really no short cut.

Money.

Boom.

I know.

You're welcome.

I love you too.

Here's the real deal, friends. There's lots of "bs" floating around out there, but there's not too many who are waving that flag of actual achievement. Stop the microwave mentality and start your crock pot mentality.

If you train yourself to fall in love with the results, you are training yourself to lose. Results are occasional. You need to start training yourself to fall in love with the process. Love the work. I train fourteen year old boys to do this when they step onto a football field. If an early teenage human can master this, I'd like to believe that you at home who actually has employment, is possibly responsible for people other than yourself, and is adulating from day to day with all the crap that is thrown at you can do this simplistic, repetitive, daily periodical thing that we all seem to make so complicated.

Let's strip this "ish" down. It's basic. It's condensed. It's primitive. But, it's so necessary for success. If you can master this technique, you are declaring your victory to the universe. Fall in love with repetition. All the great ones do it. That's how they "earn" it.

Again. Again. Again. Again. Again. Again some more. And, again wins again.

You may hate me now, but you can thank me later. Wax on. Wax off. I mean after all, I'm not doing this to *"Win Friends And Influence People."* See what I did there? Dale Carnegie? *"Win Friends And Influence People?"* A "personal growth" joke? No? First time? Oy. People.

The bottom line is that the greats have many methods of becoming and staying great, but there really isn't a substitution when we talk about what it takes to get there. Anyone handed something precious verses someone who has EARNED something precious are two total different scenarios. The latter is usually prominent for the long term.

Victory starts with one word: repeat.

## KEY 4

# DISCIPLINE (WORK ETHIC WINS)

*"Diamonds are nothing more than chunks of coal that stuck to their jobs."* — Malcolm Forbes

I, FOR ONE, do not get overly excited about the prospect of New Years Resolutions. If you do, more power to you and don't let me be the rain on your parade. Personally speaking, I think that any new month, week or even morning can be utilized as a fresh start. I try not to put too much personal stock into January first, especially if December thirty-first is going to be a real hootenanny. Listen go-getters, let's remember to enjoy life on occasions. I know all my last to leave, party rocking, party working DJ friends push all those goals to January second.

I remember when my son Kane reached his mid-teens. He followed in his father's footsteps of being what I was in my mid-teens - a total gym rat.

Pre-driver's license, I remember picking him up from his workout one cold January morning.

"How'd it go?" I asked.

"Good," he said with obligation and great disinterest.

For those of you who have not yet embraced the joy of parenting a teenager, understand that this forced, limited conversation is more than common; it is an expected lifestyle. Anything more than this can be considered as suspicious activity, concerning, and there are available hotlines and online support groups if you are in need.

"What did you work on today?" I asked. I was prying for something more in the conversation. I needed to make it worth the money spent on the gym membership that I wasn't currently using, and somehow bring gratification.

"Back, chest, legs and abs."

"Oh," I said. The urge to repeat my suggestions of how to not overtrain was interrupted by unexpected conversation.

"There were all these people in there today," He continued. "I've been going for months and I haven't seen any of them. You can tell most of them don't know what they are doing."

"No? Must be all the people with a New Years Resolu—"

"Yeah!" He said, exasperated. "I was waiting to use a bench. This guy would do his set, and when he was done, instead of getting up and letting me do my set he just laid there. I was going to tell him to get up, but the weight he was bench pressing is what I could curl, so I didn't feel like changing all of the weights."

I chimed in with, "That's so rude. Some people—"

"But then this old guy came up to me," he said (as if I wasn't speaking). He told me, "Don't worry. They'll all be gone by next week."

Well hold me down. That "old guy" who was probably pushing 28 had some pearls of wisdom right there. Why do we quit so easy? All you angry New Years Resolution people can relax. The better question actually is: Why do we sometimes never even get started? Check it out...

> "I fear not the man who has practiced 10,000 kicks once. I fear the man who has practiced one kick 10,000 times." — Bruce Lee

If you are going to be successful, you obviously have to use your head. If you plan on making a living by being the top winter coat salesman in Iraq, you may need to rethink life, or at least grab a part time gig. But what I'm talking about right here is some "good, old fashioned, in the trenches, get your hands dirty, we're gonna be here a while" work ethic. It seems like a dying art.

"I am a violinist."

Those are the words that a friend of mine who was waiting to take off on a flight couldn't help but overhear. The conversation from the people in the row behind him caught his attention. An elderly woman was sitting next to a man in his young twenties as they started some small talk. They were discussing what it was that he did for a living.

"A violinist? Oh that's fantastic" she said. "How often do you get work?"

"Well right now it's rough. I only play for one hour a week."

"Oh!" she responded. "Have you ever thought of playing with a symphony? You may be able to pull in more work—and exposure, too."

"I tried that," he said. "But I stopped doing it. When I played violin for a symphony, I felt like a worker bee. It was so annoying."

"Annoying?" she asked.

At this point it was crystal clear that this was not only a generational gap, but a mindset gap as well. Looks like the "work ethic" topic was unfortunately never a part of this young man's upbringing. The elderly woman was stunned and disgusted with this potentially starving artist. He clearly had talent. He absolutely needed an avenue but found that the one avenue that could pay revenue was to be "annoying," as this was the term he used more than once.

I can't say I disagree with her.

It's not a catchphrase, it is fact. Hard work beats talent when talent doesn't work hard. Or in this case, at all.

> *"There is no substitute for persistence…failure cannot cope with persistence."*
> — Napoleon Hill, *Think & Grow Rich*

When learning how to walk, if a baby falls forty nine times that baby doesn't think to himself "Maybe this walking thing isn't for me." Right? Right. The baby gets up the 50th and 51st and 52nd time until eventually that baby is like a kraken released from it's cage - wild and free - destroying everything in sight and making it's parents nuts.

When that baby keeps falling, nobody is standing around shouting "loser!" Even if they were and that baby be on the struggle bus, that baby is still going to work it's way through the process until it can finally get on it's two feet.

Now I've coached and watched others coach some really good players that broke my heart. They broke my heart because I would hear them say something to the effect of although they enjoy the sport that they were playing, they probably wouldn't continue at the next level (middle school, high school, college) because they "didn't want to work that hard."

It crushes me.

I've coached many a great athlete. Once in a blue moon there is that special one. I've coached some players at the middle school level who had physical attributes beyond grown men and were poised to be unstoppable monsters, as long as they didn't stop themselves. On very few occasions when I had the opportunity to work with that special kind of player, I have had to have that eye-to-eye, man-to-man, coach-to-player, father-to-son conversation.

The private powwow gets really real when I cut the opportunity for any small talk and explain to my emerging monster that there really isn't any competition that I can serve up for them at practice on the field, court, ring, chessboard, whatever. I advise that what they need to do to be challenged is to challenge that competitor in the mirror. They have to keep striving to be better, stronger, wiser, quicker, and everything else that it will take without succumbing to the temptations of just getting by on their unrivaled, raw talent.

It can be so hard for someone who is so gifted to see through the fog of their own press. That applause for what could be their fleeting moment in the sun is alluring.

I don't think that I've "heard it all," but I've definitely been around several blocks several times and have heard a lot.

"My kid could have been an NHL Player. Seriously. He was that great."

"Wow! Well, what happened?"

"He wanted to screw around, and party. Threw it all away."

Or, "That kid had a Scholarship to a D1 School for baseball."

"Amazing! How did it work out?"

"It didn't. When he got to that level he ran into competition that was just better prepared so it ended there."

Screwed around. Partied. Less prepared. Threw it all away. It's sickening.

> *"If there is no struggle there is no progress."* — Frederick Douglas

I have a friend who was a professional radio DJ for a good fifteen years. This sage has lived so much life through the different musical trends from the late 1970's disco era to the early 1990's grunge scene and everything else in between that the big, crazy '80s threw at us including rap, techno, hair bands, punk, metal, etc. He met everyone. I mean seriously. I have been on TV, worked and rubbed shoulders with the rich and famous, but this cat is still one of the few people who never ceases to impress me.

Sometimes I would sit down and throw out random performers ranging anywhere from Madonna to Bon Jovi. He would sit back and say "Oh, well one time me and (insert amazingly famous rockstar name here) were in this hotel room in L.A. breaking furniture at 3 am and I was like 'I better leave before it gets too nuts.'" I'm literally talking the stuff of legend.

But he isn't rockstar cool in his own right just because of whom he has worked, partied, and rubbed shoulders with in the industry (which would be everybody). He's rockstar cool because he gives back. He teaches and creates platforms for kids to become rockstars themselves. He urges kids to learn to play not one or two, but several instruments all while learning how to be artists by writing, composing and collaborating with other kids their age. This is all guided by young, cutting edge instructors who know how to get the most out of their students, and who are all involved in their own producing, recording and performing projects. This is different than generic music lessons where you play some chords and remember how to play "Walk This Way" by Aerosmith. Here you learn some chords, and begin to understand music theory so you can not only cover "Walk This Way" by Aerosmith, but learn to write, record, perform like and potentially be better than Aerosmith. It's ridiculously unrivaled and cool. Needless to say, this person has my attention and I am a fan.

One weeknight I walked into his monstrosity of a music haven where kids were set in their own private lesson rooms on all different floors with their respected instructors. I was dropping off my young teenager Kane who was in the process of learning piano which was his 4th learned instrument after drums, guitar and bass.

"Hey! What's going on?"

"Shhh," he said. "Listen."

He stood fixated in this arena like room watching a barefoot girl sitting on the stage. The singer was accompanied by an instructor who was softly strumming guitar, and her vocals were so melodic it made me stop in my tracks.

"See her?" he whispered. "She's amazing."

Right there with his credibility, credentials, and exposure to the business you can believe that I believed I was hearing a young lady who was in fact, amazing. He didn't take his eyes off of the performer but went on to say:

"That's a former student of mine. She just came back to say 'Hi.'"

"Oh," I said. "She is amazing!"

"Mmhmm," he murmured and slowly nodded. "If you could combine the range of Christina Aguilera, the style of Whitney Houston and the octaves of Mariah Carey, you have this girl."

Needless to say, I had nothing to say. I just had to listen. She was tremendous.

Then he added, "And she'll never make it."

"Mmhmm," I said. "Wait. What? Why?"

"You know why," he said sternly as he moved his eyes off of the stage to look at me for the first time in our conversation.

"Work ethic."

"Hold on" I said. "You just told me she could be the greatest woman vocal ever and—"

"I know what I said," he affirmed (he's got a way with people). "But, I'm telling you, you know what it takes to make it, and she doesn't have it. She'd rather screw around with some part time stuff instead of really getting serious and doing what it takes to make it to the next level. She should be on your radio, but she'll be waiting tables, and it breaks my heart."

Wow. Disappointed but not surprised, I've heard it before. You've read it just a few paragraphs back—hard work beats talent when talent doesn't work hard. Do you know why? It's because when the talented, potential superstars who are the total package get tired, want to party or figure that they don't really want it that bad after all, they'll quit.

But, someone who may have a third of the talent who had to fight for everything that they have—someone who has the range of Christina Aguilera - but doesn't necessarily have the style of Whitney Houston or the octaves of Mariah Carey is out there. And they're hungry. That person will hang around when everyone else has left. They're tired and broke, but they will not quit. They won't go home until they've won. The ones who really want it don't stop when they get tired. They stop when the job is done.

Losers focus on pleasing activities. Winners focus on pleasing results. The ones who win are disciplined enough to focus on the results that they want by putting in the work.

*"I can accept failure, everyone fails at something. But I can't accept not trying."* — Michael Jordan

Check this out. If somebody has ever targeted you as a "Try Hard," that means they've identified you as a person who is a teacher's pet, the kid who may not be the next superstar athlete but comes out for the team anyhow yet never says die, or the one who is just a little "extra." They didn't mean to, but in a backhanded way they've actually given you a compliment.

When I was a kid, I went to school with some "Try Hards." They were total "nerds." Today? Today those "Try Hards" and "nerds" are CEOs. They are the ones who cut paychecks for the once kids who were too cool to go all out and now have grown up to become part of the herd.

The "Try Hards" are partners of their lawn firms. They are professional athletes. They are entrepreneurs who have created a life by design. They are absolutely people who have that grit, and most importantly the attitude that is exactly what is needed to make it in times like these.

Ever hear the expression "Lions don't lose sleep over the opinions of sheep?"

Please. Identify and call the ones who go for it "Try Hards." I hope they don't care about the opinions of others. I hope they find pleasure in outworking the talented and privileged ones. I hope they find comfort in that sweet spot of grinding out their talent and passion in private so the world can celebrate them in public.

I hope that for you, too. Be that "Try Hard." Be that guy, that girl, that extra one who won't quit, won't stop, and won't go away. Be that one who is creating their own success, despite being the punchline while hearing the laughter and insults over and over. Keep going. The ones laughing? Remember them. Remember who they are so when they ask permission to enter your office you can decide if you feel like seeing them now - or ever. Decide how much or how little money you want to give them for a raise, or how many days granted leave for vacation - if granted at all.

Here's to you in the trenches my nerdy, try hard friends. Stay on pace. You WILL be making a difference before you know it.

> *"Opportunity is missed by most people because it is dressed like overalls and looks like work."* — Thomas Edison

I tell people success is like ordering a pizza. Then, they look at me like I'm an idiot. So, I feel compelled to explain. Just like now.

Say you're hanging out with friends and you get hungry. You order a pizza. Thirty minutes later the delivery guy rings your doorbell, and now you have a fresh, delicious, piping hot pizza. Mmmm. Pizza.

You eat some slices. Maybe you save some for later. Maybe there's none left. It doesn't really matter. It came and went and now you're onto the next thing.

What you didn't see (and probably don't care about) is what it took for you to get that pizza. You didn't see the old man who was kneading the dough and meticulously spreading the sauce evenly before you even thought to call in your order. The girl in the worn tank top with a ponytail who took your order over the phone had three people standing in line staring at her with at least two other lines on hold, all while you put her on hold to debate with your friend whether or not she should add pepperoni.

You also didn't even think about the guy with the five o'clock shadow. He's in a t-shirt covered by a sauce stained apron. He's sweating in that kitchen, pulling your pizza out of the hot oven with his wooden pie spatula, sliding it perfectly into the cardboard box. That's one of the fifty boxes that the new employee high school kid spent an hour making when he first got there for his shift.

Timmy the delivery guy? He has seven stops. He's stressed. It's Friday night, traffic is heavy and his boss who owns the shop (the old man who kneads the dough and spreads the sauce) is all over him to not chit-chat and get back quickly because food is getting cold and customers are getting angry. If he has to remind Timmy to move faster one more time, Timmy may have to go get a job somewhere else. Maybe Target. Who cares? Just hurry back.

You tipped Timmy two dollars.

I'm not trying to dramatically guilt you because you didn't thank the universe for the high school kid who stacked the cardboard pizza boxes. I am trying to make a comparison showing you that we view success just like how we order a pizza.

So many times we forget ourselves and just expect. We make the call and it's a no brainer that we'll simply have it, right? We tend to look at the end product and sometimes we never see that back kitchen. It doesn't occur to us to consider all the hands, the time, the effort, the coordination, the work. We just want the pizza.

This isn't a call to action for you to start a prayer chain with friends from church, or list your pizza at the top spot in your gratitude journal. But, if we had to knead our own dough, pour the sauce, sweat in that kitchen, take our own call with a line full of hostile customers staring at us, build the cardboard box, and fight through traffic to drive that Sicilian masterpiece to our home all by ourselves, would we ever actually put in the effort? Wouldn't we just throw something in the microwave instead? Bagel Bites sound pretty good to me. Either that or I say grab a Lean Cuisine.

It's always been like this, but it's gotten even worse in our microwave mentality society. Many want the success. Many want the title. Many want the money. In this case many want the pizza. Few will work for it.

You might view this fact as sad, but I see it as offering hope. It's hopeful because you can see the trend. You can know what to expect and you can prepare accordingly. If you can separate yourself from the "give up easy herd" by making a decision to be on purpose, you're on the right track. If you expect things to get rough, you're even more prepared. If you expect things to get rough but know that you are plowing forward no matter what—I said—*no matter what*, then you can start to be taken seriously.

That's the blueprint, and it should get you excited. The winners reading this just felt a shot of adrenaline. Maybe their blood pumped a little harder. Some people just woke up. Are you that someone I am writing about?

*"Depend on the rabbit's foot if you will, but remember it didn't work for the rabbit."* — R. E. Shay

Lucky and free. That sounds so refreshing doesn't it? Who doesn't want to be lucky? Who doesn't want to be free? I subscribe to the theory that the harder I work, the luckier I get.

There are no overnight success stories. You hear of the fame and see the success, but you didn't witness the backstory. You didn't see the years of dreams, work, rejection, tears, and the tenacity of fighting for it all. You just see that person who got lucky.

And I hope you get lucky.

I hope you are lucky enough to never be privileged and never have things handed to you early on. I hope there are times in your life where there is discomfort; when you are picked last; when you are ignored; when you are laughed at.

I hope you are so lucky that you don't have things handed to you so you become soft, comfortable and ineffective. I hope you get to earn your way onto the field. I hope you get that starting role, position, and raise because you deserve it, not because you knew somebody who could have you leapfrog the line in front of you. I hope you get lucky enough to know what desperation can feel like, and the electrifying, saving gratitude of when you make it through to the other side.

I hope you have to take a backseat, ride the bench, and chase after what you want. I hope for your sake, you are lucky enough to experience this so you can learn and know what it will require for you to dig so deep to get off of that bench and out from that backseat.

The same people that want to get lucky are also the ones who desire things they can get for free. There are so many things that are free to you right now, and it doesn't matter how much skill or talent you have for you to utilize them.

Effort is free. A little effort goes a long way because actions are stronger than words. You can put effort into yourself, your goal, your dream right now and it wouldn't cost you a dime. But, the payoff would be huge.

Preparation is free. You can prepare as much as you do or don't want. Just know this: the ones who put in the effort of preparing, the really prepared ones? They seem to win, don't they? They prepared without cost.

You won't get charged for passion. You may be rewarded for it, and you will absolutely get noticed because of it, but it won't cost you anything.

If you want to get lucky, your energy is required. The thing about energy is that it will get low. The good news is that you have a never-ending supply that will recharge and build itself back up. You can never run out. So, your energy? It's endless and free for you to use anytime you want.

Your attitude is priceless and it's always complimentary. The better the attitude, the more charmed your life will be. Attitude is crucial to your being. That's why I dedicated a whole chapter to it.

You already realize that you have been, are, and will be judged by others. They are able to tell how much you weigh, how fast you can run, how much money you have and what your intelligence quotient or IQ is. One day you're going to realize something else, too. Those people? The ones who judge you? You are going to learn that they will never be able to measure your heart. Only you can do that.

Don't give up. I have hope for you. My hope is that you are wise enough to not squander these things that are free to you. I hope you really utilize your effort and preparation. I hope you take that energy and passion and squeeze every once out of it. I really hope you use that attitude so it will benefit you and create some great things in your life.

Most of all, I hope you never do give up on those things that are important to you. I hope you receive that great gift of having to earn your way. The feeling of knowing that you've truly accomplished something because of your sweat equity is priceless.

The greatest edge of all that can never be taken away from you, is the knowledge that you used everything available to you and you won with it. Go win with all of those free tools that are available to you so one day you will be the one they are talking about.

How rewarding it will be when you have them scratching their heads wondering how you always seem to just get so "lucky."

RANT #5

# CONTROL

*"You have brains in your head. You have feet in your shoes. You can steer yourself any direction you choose."* — Dr. Seuss, *Oh, the Places You'll Go!*

**HERE'S A NEWS** flash for you: your goals don't care about your feelings.

Whoa. Pretty harsh, dude.

I know. And for the record, when you are done with this book you will know that I am pretty big on feeling, emotion, energy, and vision. But we're not talking about me. We're talking about your goals. And your goals don't care about what you feel. Your goals care about results.

I grew up hearing my combat trained, Vietnam veteran father speak of the importance of discipline constantly. This is why I have such an appreciation for it.

If you were to look up "discipline" in the *Merriam-Webster Dictionary*, you would read:

A) Control gained by enforcing obedience or order.
B) Orderly or prescribed conduct or pattern of behavior.
C) Self control.

Someone that I've coached with for years is John Morgenthaler. John is great. He's the guy who is always just one moment away from bursting with emotion, having veins pop out of his neck, and yelling instructions with eyes wide as saucers. But when this is happening he's always building the kids up. He never tears them down. The kids absolutely love this man, and he completely loves them back.

This past summer we held a defensive coaches meeting and John admitted to us that it was his thirtieth year of being sober. He hasn't touched a drop of alcohol since the 1980s. He recalled being at a party one night while right then and there he pushed away a pitcher of beer. He wanted to find out who was the boss: him or that pitcher of beer.

John won. And he has continued to win ever since simply because of his mental fortitude. He has discipline.

Jeff Bezos? You know...the guy who built Amazon to be the most mammoth retail beast in the galaxy? Yeah, that guy. Let's round up to say his net worth is a cool 111 billion dollars. I said billion with a "b." Like bagel. Or bad boy. Or Bolivia. 111 billion.

Bezos is known for his unmatched work ethic where stories date even back to his high school days. A former classmate recalled a story that when Bezos had made it perfectly clear that he intended to be high school valedictorian, "everyone else understood they were working for second place."

After launching Amazon, twelve hour days, seven days a week, sometimes staying up working until 2 or 3 am shipping books was the norm. That doesn't take a good feeling. That takes discipline. I'm sure the couch looked comfy, a nap was needed, and a break would be nice. But do you want to be number one, or do you want to take a nap? Discipline.

If you read *"Get Up"* you may recall Chapter two named "Success, Failure, And What We Tell Ourselves." The fictional character in that chapter named "Andy" was inspired by a family friend named Alex Rosano (or A-Rose). Over the last few years I've had people ask me what happened to "Andy." Andy (or Alex) has moved on to play college football. But when I talked about how "Andy" could possibly make it to the NBA, I didn't just make it up. I had a blueprint for it. Allow me to introduce you to that blueprint.

"Larry Legend," number 33, and better known to you as Larry Bird is in the conversation of being arguably the best passing and shooting forward in the history of the National Basketball Association. He was automatic but had an early reputation for being a mediocre, slow defender. He wasn't necessarily known for a ton of talent. He was known for his discipline.

As a sophomore in high school he had a broken ankle. He also had a relentless work ethic. Propping himself on crutches, every single day at 6am he would shoot a minimum of 500 free throws. Not 100. Not 300. 500.

A high school coach told him there was more to being good than just shooting. Bird (who was right handed) began to practice dribbling with his left hand. Constantly. Sitting with friends, walking around, warming up—all left handed.

When Bird played with the Boston Celtics he won 3 NBA Titles, was an All-Star 12 times, won three straight regular-season Most Valuable Player awards, and was the NBA Finals MVP twice. That wasn't luck. That was work.

Discipline is the founding father of success. You can have it. It's a decision. Decide to do it when you don't "feel" like it. Screw your feelings. When you must get it done, when you have to get over the hump, and unquestionably when you need to make a change, discipline is supreme.

Like the Nike slogan "Just Do It." Again, your goals don't care about your feelings. Make an excuse or make it happen. You decide.

# KEY 5

# MOTIVATION (HIGH ENERGY)

*"To find yourself, think for yourself."* — Socrates

**AS WE ARE** midway into this utterly bombastic and ridiculously groundbreaking paperback, I refuse to go any further without dousing out a mini-firestorm. There's a recent myth that needs to be knocked into nonexistence before people—educated people with good intentions—start believing this jibber jabber, jive turkey talk.

Now clearly from the last pages that you've read you understand my feelings on the much needed attribute of discipline. But what we're talking about here, friends, is the notion that motivation is worthless.

Worthless? Hmmm.

This trend started somewhere around 2017-18 where a handful of the "experts" of the day started proclaiming this and tossing it around like glitter in a nightclub. Being referred to as a motivational speaker became somewhat taboo. I saw the authors and motivational speakers...um, or whatever they are called now, get on interviews and write in their books about how motivation/inspiration is trash.

According to the circle of ones who have a platform, motivation is insignificant and the real key to success is discipline. More on that in a moment. I've heard one speaker imply that motivation is meaningless because "it comes and goes." I'll get to that in uno momento as well.

But with a few books mentioning it, and some interviews talking about it (Ah, the internet) - boom! We're off! Just like that the anti-motivation campaign was born.

Then I started noticing many people on social media who started making their home-grown "Facebook Lives" and "Watch Parties" intending to give their thoughts on this matter. Most would drop the same tone. I don't want to say they were being "sheople" or repeating this anti-motivation notion like parrots. I just think most didn't really look at it from a full perspective. And once again let's hear it for the internet! The slogan should read "The world wide web: where everyone can have a voice. Even if they're wrong."

Look, when you see "experts" push a thought when the machine is backing them it's easy to be enamored with them and their ideas. "They" think it's right so it has to be right. Right? Weeell...I guess I'm the guy who has this radical idea that the expert's radical idea on this topic is hot trash, and maybe we should start thinking for ourselves. Friends, there are 7.8 billion people in the world. Don't let the opinion of one or two sway you into not being an independent thinker.

> *"Motivation is crap. Motivation comes and goes."* — David Goggins

Okay. My turn.

I hate to be the lone party-pooper but I'm a little confused by this trend. And quite frankly this author and motivational speaker (call me what you will) thinks that the idea of motivation being garbage is garbage.

Please allow me to list the ways in which I think this is a halfcocked, shortsighted perspective. I will now present an argument which may have you leaving this chapter with a new appreciation for the aforementioned useless emotion of motivation.

"Motivation is crap" because it "comes and goes." Wowzers. That's some profound talk right there. "Wooowee," I say. As a matter of fact that's not only as deep as the ocean is blue, it's just downright outrageous. And if you think about it, it really doesn't any make sense whatsoever.

Everything comes and goes. You just use as much of it as you can to your benefit when it is there.

You know. Daytime? Yep. It's here. Again. Everyday. It doesn't mean it's crap, useless or unimportant, but you better believe I'm going to make the most of it when it gets here. I need a tan. Let's hit the beach!

Wait. It's nighttime? Again? Let's party! Again. Better yet, let's go to sleep. Well come to think of it sleep comes and goes too, so it must be useless as well.

The trash and recycling guys? Whoah. They only show up once a week. They must be really useless! But I have a heaping curbside pickup for them when they do. Hold up. What about that every once and a while when I need them for "bulk day?"

Your birthday. Holy moly. Once a year! I personally have only had the chance to celebrate it forty-eight times so far, so there better be some sweet presents when I do it for the forty-ninth. But who's counting?

So like all the major things in life—sunlight, your birthday, trash pickup—they come and go. The great Jim Rohn once said, "Motivation is like bathing. It wears off. That's why we recommend it daily."

> "I have not yet begun to fight!" — John Paul Jones

My football players already have discipline. They've already put in the work. They've been training hard. They show up on the field dressed like gladiators and are ready to block, tackle, and everything else that they need to do at high speeds. For most of them, it will most likely be the most physical activity that they've ever performed in their lives. That's mental toughness. That's discipline.

So for the record football players have discipline. Check. They need it. Without it they go nowhere, are stopped in their tracks, and it's the end of this conversation. It's both mentally and physically exhausting to show up to football practice everyday. But they do. Now, here comes the motivation.

We want them to get to the next layer. We want them to level up.

Game day is special. You go to bed the night before dreaming about it just like you do when it's Christmas Eve. You wake up with a spring in your step. You get to wear your jersey to school. Everyone can see that you are a part of this elite team and that you are representing them. There is electricity in the air!

Now it's pre-game warmups and the opposing team rolls into our guest parking lot two school buses deep. Their cleats hit our ground, walk onto our field, and warm up in our end-zone. It would be best for them if they climbed back on the bus and went back to wherever they came from before we hurt some feelings and *send* them back on the bus to wherever they came from.

This is our house. Our home. We've put in all the hard work right here where we stand. We've been running hills. We've been sweating our faces off. We've been tearing each other apart preparing. For this. This moment. Right now. Our parents, girlfriends, friends, community, and FAMILY are here to watch. WE are a family. WE have each other's backs. And they - THEY - think that they're just going to come in here and TAKE it all? From US? Not a chance. Our hard work, our dedication, our dignity is on the line. Not today.

You feel that? Is your blood pumping? Are you breathing just a little harder? I am. Is the hair standing up on the back of your neck? How do you think the players feel? They're the ones actually living it. They just needed to be gently reminded why they've put in all that hard work.

That. They feel that.

That's motivation.

Now my already disciplined team is hype, too. And they are ready to make that discipline pay off. They can climb to another level easily with that adrenaline from the motivation. This emotionally charged squad is so motivated that by the time that whistle blows for kickoff, these young gladiators will be ready to run through a flaming, barb wired brick wall if need be. That's when I cut our dogs loose, and you don't want to be wearing that other colored jersey.

> "What's the point of insulting each other? The Garden is sold out, that's why!" — Muhammad Ali

Motivation is about an energy. Motivation inspires action and action gets things done. If you were to look in a thesaurus for synonyms of motivation you would see words like spark, galvanize, excite, inspire, arouse, quicken, fire. Who doesn't want some of that? I know I do. You don't? Big fat liar, liar, pants on fire, you.

I live next to nothing. Nothing. It's like that song by Journey. You know. "Stree-eet lights. Peo-ple. Whoa-oh-ooooooooooooh." Yeah we don't have any of that. There's no street lights. There's no people. There's nothing. And I am a master of forgetting my wallet when I leave to run errands. I usually find out at about the 20 to 25 minute mark of being en route to my destinations. So I'm either really out getting everything done or I'm really home with no intention of making the trek to civilization.

That is of course unless I'm hungry. Then let's take a nice forty-five minute drive over to our favorite place and grab that sushi real quick. Because nothing says sushi like an hour and a half round trip.

I'm motivated. By food. That's how you train animals. From dogs to dolphins they are motivated to respond to the treat they are going to receive. The trainer didn't discipline that dolphin. The trainer fed that dolphin. That dolphin learned it would get rewarded for doing what the trainer wanted. It was motivated to react a certain way so it could receive a certain reward.

Why did people buy tickets to see Muhammad Ali fight in the 1960s and 70s? They either wanted to see him get his mouth shut or talk that jive talk when he didn't. They wanted to be a part of it. That want motivated them to fill up the seats and sell out Madison Square Garden. Again.

A girl flirting with a guy motivates that guy to ask that girl out, actually drive to pick her up, and bring her somewhere on a date. If he's really motivated he may possibly stop somewhere along the way to purchase her flowers or a gift. That kid has zero discipline. He skipped out on two college classes, put beer and ramen noodles on his credit card, and texted the whole way while driving to her house. But he's making moves. He's motivated. Playa.

A great movie trailer motivates people to buy their ticket online, leave their home, and go watch it in the theatre before it hits Netflix. Not all those moviegoers are disciplined. As a matter of fact they reacted with a lack of discipline. They couldn't even wait a few months. They needed to see it right now. Are they a pack of bozos or did they just respond to a call to action?

A floundering sales team gets inspired with a bangin' incentive and now they're all over it. They're selling their faces off. They already knew what to do. Maybe they were already doing it. Now they're just *really* doing it!

Again friends, Hayford's not trippin' trying to put the bad mouth on discipline. I was raised with it. I'm just trying to get the "motivation is crap" camp to stop throwing shade on motivation and see the positives in it. Discipline had nothing to do with any of the results that I've just showcased, but motivation did.

Motivation is important because inspired people get things done. Together a lot of inspired people will get a lot of things done. So it's okay. Be motivated. Get pumped up. Go be inspired. Stand and cheer. Run that marathon. Crush those goals.

Then be thankful that at some point the adrenaline will subside. It needs to so you can sleep well tonight and have the energy to do whatever it is that you do all over again tomorrow. Enjoy that motivation when it's here just like the sunshine, the recycling guy, and your birthday.

## RANT #6

# GET MOVING

*"Movement is a privilege."* — Dr. Darren Rodia / CEO & founder of Kinetic Physical Therapy (2015's #1 American Physical Therapy Practice Of The Year)

THIS RANT ISN'T about goals and dreams, achieving or attacking life. This is about admitting that sometimes everything is so unbearably heavy.

I know sometimes the gloom can drape itself around us like a wet blanket. Laying in bed numb or scrolling until whenever is so much easier than taking a first step. It's easier to accept and just exist. Maybe things will get better by themselves. Or not. It's cumbersome. Daunting. Depressing.

Your funk. That rut. We need to—no, YOU need to get yourself out of it. I know you know that. I also know that it's easier said than done.

Have you ever been in the situation where you were going to go to the gym, or church, a party, the store, whatever, and you had zero ambition or drive to go? You didn't feel like it? Of course you have. Have you ever been in that situation and somehow went anyway? How did that make you feel? Weren't you happy once you've arrived there? You weren't only content because you created a small victory by just showing up but it probably wasn't as bad as the mind initially made it out to be. Most people don't feel like doing most things unless those things bring pleasure. Most people don't feel like doing the things that can create success. That's why most people aren't successful. They allow their feelings to run the show. I have some advice and I hope you don't take this the wrong way.

Screw your feelings! Not always but when they get in the way of you simply functioning it's time to shake things up.

Depression is real. So is this. This one isn't about motivation. This is about fact. Motion creates motion. Opportunity creates opportunity. Activity cures all. You need to get moving.

Brian Tracy wrote a book called *"Eat That Frog."* Who wants to eat a live frog? Nobody. That's a terrible idea. It's probably one of the worst things you can do. That's why you do it first thing in the day. If you were to eat a live frog everything else after that would be easy.

Mel Robbins created the *"Five Second Rule"* where your feelings don't get a say. 5, 4, 3, 2, 1, and go. Like Nike, just do it. It has helped thousands but it all just sounds too simplistic, right?

Okay, how about the other Robbins? Tony. He is really big on changing your physiology. That's why there is so much movement in his seminars. We were meant to move. Our ancestors were masters at it and yet many of us just don't anymore. Too much sitting. Too much laying. Too much bleb. It creates a mood. Changing your physiology in certain moments will change your perspective which will change your actions and ultimately change your life!

Listen. You need to stand. Literally. Physically stand up. Or go for a walk, do push-ups, change your breathing to rapid, run as fast as you can for 30 seconds, or as ridiculous as it sounds, do a jumping jack. Clap your hands. Flex your muscles. Sing your favorite song—loudly. Yell out "YES"! Nod your head yes to this right now.

Motion does create motion. Motion also creates emotion. Your funk and your rut ends here. I'll remind you again that you are in total control. A great first step to seizing that control is to start moving. Choose it. You will not be sorry. Take one step, one baby step. Do one thing. Just get started. A wise man (or at least a handsome one) once said "Get Up"!

# KEY 6

# COURAGE (HACKING FEAR)

*"Too many of us are not living our dreams because we are living our fears."* — Les Brown

**ON DECEMBER 16TH, 2018** (my birthday) I released my second book *"365 Days Of Encouraging You To Attack Life."* Like it's predecessor "Get Up," "365" shot to the number one spot at the top of the Amazon's "Self Help" category. It didn't smash records and get there in under four hours like *"Get Up"* did, but it still hit the number one spot in just one day. What a great birthday present that was!

Then I noticed something pretty cool that started to happen. The daily encouragement book "365" started to creep up in other category charts such as "Neurolinguistic

Programming" or "NLP." It also registered on the "Anxieties & Phobias" category.

Wait. What? There's actually an "Anxieties & Phobias" category? That's a thing?? Unfortunately, yes.

Fear. It's like the mailman. Or wintertime. You can expect it to show up; sometimes even consistently. I always refer to the acronym of fear as being "false evidence appearing real." Unfortunately for most it appears all too real, all too much, all too often.

Something became so fascinating to me as I researched various sources. I've explored information, statistics and studies ranging from CNBC to the American Psychiatric Association. I've spoken with teenagers who have been victimized by self doubt when either they or their parents have reached out to me through Snapchat or Instagram. I've read articles that were spawned by programs from Oxford University. I've reached the end of the internet. I even witnessed the overwhelming anxiety exhibited by my nerdy tech friend George when it's his turn to make another indecisive pick at our fantasy football draft. Oh, George.

Conclusion to all studies is this: We as people are absolutely petrified.

I don't need to be Captain Obvious and tell you what you already know. Grown men, teenagers, professional athletes, CEOs of companies, housewives and everyone else under the sun all have some type of angst or anxiety.

There are so many fears and phobias, it is actually as fascinating as it is ridiculous. I'm not trying to exaggerate, I'm being pragmatic. We all know some of the most common fears which include the fear of death, public speaking (which is actually ranked over death), heights, germs, fear of spiders or arachnophobia (you can lump other bugs in there as well), dogs, snakes, money (or lack of), corrupt government officials, sharks (same thing as corrupt government officials), claustrophobia, needles, lighting, and thanks to Steven King's "It"...clowns.

My wife? She prays on elevators. As in she prays going from the fourth floor to the lobby. Out loud. That is of course, unless she decides to take the stairs. I always meet her in the lobby—that's right—from the elevator. One time I pointed out to her that the issue wasn't the elevator. The issue was her. Well, we all make mistakes. The conversation following that statement didn't turn out to be a top ten "fun" moment in my life. C'mon though. In the off chance that anyone actually does happen to get stuck in an elevator, we've all seen enough Bruce Willis movies to know that not only can we escape but we just might be able to save the world while doing it, too.

Fear of flying is a big one. That makes sense too, right? You are screaming through the sky hundreds of miles an hour all while being captive in this metal contraption that is propelling thousands of feet above the ground. But even though this could cause angst it is guesstimated that there is a one to somewhere between a five to eleven million chance that your plane actually goes down. You are more likely to be struck by lightning, attacked by a shark, or killed walking down the street than being involved in a plane crash!

Then there are some of the less common - or should we not be so politically correct and just lay it all out there - downright strange phobias. Raise your hand if you are a weirdo and suffer from Genuphobia. You know. The fear of knees. Yes, knees: as in what's between your ankles and hips.

Any of you freakazoids out there worried about Octophobia? What's that? Oh, it's just the fear of the number eight. Not six. Not seven. Eight. And that's weird because I've always been taught that six was afraid of seven because seven ate nine. Seven ate nine? Gotcha. I'm dying right now. Can't even help it.

Moving on, who doesn't walk around trembling from Aulophobia? Obviously (duh) that's the fear of flutes which is so different from ishicascadiggaphobia. I can't even pronounce that, but it's clearly the fear of elbows. Elbows? Freakin' elbows. I mean some of these are incredibly ridiculous. Don't even get me started on zombies.

Recently I saw something in passing (I believe on the negative nelly nerve wracking news) regarding a "Doomsday Clock." So there's a Doomsday Clock? And it made the news? Now I don't pay too much mind to that nonsense but I find it very telling that many people do.

What's the point to all of this? The point is the mind can hijack us into a fearful, paralyzed state if we choose to let it take over and run wild. And what do we typically tend to do when that happens? Absolutely nothing. We freeze. Or worse. We obsess. So what can we do about it? Well, let's take a closer look.

*"You're gonna need a bigger boat."*
— Roy Scheider (from the 1975 movie *"Jaws"*)

You want fear? I'll show you fear. Try walking a mile in my shoes. Or better yet walk a hundred yards in them from the field to the locker room. As I mentioned earlier in this modern day classic I'm a football coach. Way before COVID-19 was ever considered a thing, going into a middle school football locker room midseason was pretty much rolling the dice with your life. It smells like barnyard animal, it's unpleasantly loud, and there's a pretty high chance that by touching anyone or anything at any given time, you're catching some kind of incurable disease. So friends, be afraid. Be very afraid.

Actually I'm exaggerating. And where most of you just groaned or gave a wince, I'm pretty okay with all of everything that I just described. The fear I personally deal with has nothing to do with middle school locker rooms or germs. It has everything to do with deep water. I mean I'm good on a boat. I can go on a cruise. I will be in a pool (by the edge). And I will go play with the waves in the ocean, that is as long as my feet can touch the sand.

You want me to cage fight a pack of wolves? Check. Come here, puppy. High speed? High altitude? High speed at high altitude? No problemo. Get me on that jet. Put me in a dark, "haunted" house? Brother, please. I have Jesus.

But swimming? Well let's just say that if you throw me in the middle of an ocean, I may be voted most likely to drown. I can swim. Kind of. Well, not really. I mean...I have before...just not so well. Aquaman I am not, even if I do constantly get mistaken for his stunt double. I take it all in stride.

Me not wanting to hurl myself off the diving board like a soon to be waterlogged, flying squirrel is logical. My "fear" of deep water is not logical. I think it has something to do with the fact that I know there are living creatures in there that can actually digest me. Oh, yeah. I almost forgot. The fact that I usually can't see them either doesn't seem to help. Let's be honest. I don't *really* know what's down there. But in saying all of this I've never actually had any terrible experiences with water that comes to mind. Security camera footage from a drugstore robbery from the 1990s is clearer to me than the reason as to why I am uncomfortable with the deep, blue sea. Nonetheless, deep water just seems to make me nervous. I'm okay with this because the remedy doesn't have to be hypnosis, an intervention, or Navy Seal training lessons. I just don't frequent deep water all that much. Solved!

One time someone said to me "My shoulder hurts when I do this..."

I said "Don't do that. Your shoulder won't hurt." Makes sense. I can enjoy the ocean up to my knees, I just don't need to scuba dive.

Regardless of my personal aquatic hangups, you've read earlier in this book that most people tiptoe through life trying to safely make it to death. You've heard "yolo" or "You only live once once." The snarky answer to that is "You only die once, too." Yeah. Ha-ha. Ha-ha-ha. Ha-ha-ha-ha-ha. Very clever! But bruh, if you're constantly hiding under the covers draped by a blanket of fear you are never, ever really living in the first place.

You've got to keep this emotion in check and take control over it or it will ruin your life. Read that again. You've got to keep this emotion in check and take control over it or it will ruin your life.

Well, that's great. But...how? Let's explore some ideas.

> *"No man is fit to command another that cannot command himself."* — William Penn

There's an adage that declares that you may not remember what someone said to you but you will remember how they made you feel. In this next particular instance I actually remember what someone said to me.

I was a kid in the 1980s. And as we usually were, my friend and then classmate Bobby Zaunczkowski and I were on the phone. For starters let's keep this easy. Call him Bobby Z. So me and Z, we were on the phone. You know… talking, because texting was about 20 years away in the future. Obviously since this was taking place about thirty five years ago in the past I was most likely stuck to the wall because of the phone cord. Or maybe I was hiding in the closet or the bathroom for privacy since I could only go as far as three foot cord would let me. Three feet. Max. Talk about social distancing. Try having a phone conversation in the 80's. You couldn't move until the call was over. How's that for a quarantine? The weird part about it was nobody seemed to notice or mind. Oh how we have evolved.

Anyhow I don't remember what we were specifically talking about, what spawned the conversation, or how we came to it. And I can bet that when he reads this he won't have any clue as to what the heck I'm even referring to in the first place. But for some reason we were talking about being stressed out. I don't remember who was stressed out, or what we were stressed out about in the first place. Maybe it was about the book report that was due for Ms. Persico's class. Maybe it was the fact that anything was due for Ms. Persico's class. It could have leaned more toward the fact that she couldn't stand either one of us. Maybe my "Men At Work" cassette tape was eaten by my Sony Walkman. Maybe I was stressed that somebody would find out that I secretly listened to Men At Work on my Sony Walkman. And you thought the 80's were all fun.

Note to self. Teens and preteens always have and probably always will have some sort of anxiety. Yes even in the longest weekend ever (which most people may recognize as): the 1980s.

Z basically told me that when he had trouble sleeping because of something that was worrying him, he would remind himself that there was nothing—absolutely nothing - that he would be able to do about it in that moment to fix whatever the problem was. In that moment he would DECIDE to simply let it go. He would put it on a shelf, worry about it some other time, forget about it, whatever. That's the moment when he would be able to get on with having a peaceful night's sleep.

Wow. I've never forgotten that and have had decades of restful nights ever since, even in times when it wasn't always smooth sailing. Pretty profound for a fourteen year old who needed to get back to his Atari and Motley Crue cassette tapes. Thanks, Z. Free, signed copy coming your way.

This method obviously isn't fixing whatever the problem is, but it is a fantastic example of making a decision of taking control of your mind and your emotions (not to mention getting a good night's rest). I've made reference in "*Get Up*" to comparing your mind to a horse in the wild. You can ride the horse. But if it's not broken in and controlled, you are getting thrashed around, thrown off, and hurt. Break that wild horse in, train it, and it will become an asset. It's powerful. It's limitless. It makes life easier.

> "Stop being afraid of what could go wrong and start being excited about what could go right." — Tony Robbins

I've seen Tony Robbins live. Going to one of his events is like being at a rock concert, legit. He brings the energy. He goes nonstop for hours upon hours, and somehow he keeps that energy level at a consistent pace for the entire time. When you leave you are exhausted yet somehow on overdrive all while knowing that what you have just experienced was worth every penny. Anyone reading this that has been to one of his events is (I'm sure) in agreement with me.

He tells a tremendous story of sidestepping fear and manipulating it to becoming a benefit. He speaks on harnessing the emotion. As a music fan I particularly enjoy this little ditty. And, no. It's not about "Jack And Diane."

Back in the day as Tony was emerging as the most renowned speaker in the world, he received a call from 1970's music star Carly Simon. Now I must tell you that today when I recite this lesson on managing fear and I'm dealing with auditoriums of high schoolers, I have to put this in a perspective that they can understand. I explain that Carly Simon was not so much, but kind of, like the Taylor Swift of the 1970s. Then I get a collection of head nods and I know that they know what I'm talking about.

As I was saying…Tony Robbins received a call from Carly Simon who has been charting songs for years and at the time was a recognizable name in the music world. She proceeded to request help from Tony explaining that she could no longer perform in front of live audiences because according to her she has acquired an overwhelming case of stage fright.

Robbins being perplexed, dug deeper, asking for her to explain her symptoms so he could get to the root of her issue. Carly (I'm paraphrasing) explained that when she peeked through the curtains and saw all those people in the crowd, it would start to happen. Her heart would start to pound in her chest so hard it felt like a heart attack. Her throat would get so tight it felt like it was closing up and that she wouldn't be able to sing. Her hands would get so sweaty it felt like she was going to drop the microphone. This is the point when Carly realized that she was having a panic attack.

Without going into great detail Tony explained that he helped her work it all out as to where she had been able to go on to perform and record and continue her musical career which spans almost five decades!

Times passes and Tony befriends Bruce Springsteen. Bruce Springsteen as in "Born To Run," "Glory Days," "Born In The USA," or the man simply know as "The Boss." Bruce is in the Rock And Roll Hall Of Fame, and Springsteen is an iconic rocker who (before Tony Robbins ever was) has been known for putting on marathon shows. Four to four-and-a-half hour concerts with original songs, anthems, covers, stories, and a total party is what he's been serving up for respectively, the past fifty years. The dude played a Super Bowl Half Time!

One year Tony was a guest of Bruce's at one of his amazing concerts. The music. The passion. The energy.

It was contagious and impressive. After the show Tony recalled how he was mentioning to Bruce that there had to be close to fifty thousand in the arena that particular night. With the accumulation of all of those people from all of those shows from one concert tour alone Bruce would easily perform to at least a million people in a calendar year.

He asked Springsteen what that felt like.

The Boss explained that (again, I'm paraphrasing) when he peeked through the curtains and saw all those people in the crowd it would start to happen. His heart would start to pound in his chest so hard it felt like a heart attack. His throat would get so tight it felt like it was closing up and that he wouldn't be able to sing. His hands would get so sweaty it felt like he was going to drop his guitar.

This is the point when Bruce knew that he was "ready."

Cool story, bro. But hold on. We just had two people who were in two similar scenarios experiencing the exact, same symptoms. One was having such a "panic attack" that she couldn't perform and the other one was so excited that he was "ready."

Who was right? Interestingly enough, they both were. And this doesn't have to do with opinions, this has to do with physiology and biology. More specifically this has everything to do with how your brain works.

> "Fears are nothing but a state of mind."
> — Napoleon Hill

In school they taught so many kinds of "ologies." You know. Biology. Sociology. Theology. I didn't like any kind of "ology." I liked LL Cool J and Van Halen. And they never taught any of it right anyway because so many of these studies are so compelling but when you don't flavor the food it may be bland. Right? Right.

Without too much yakety-yak let's get down to business and see exactly why your brain acts the way it does in the face of fear and what you can do about it. Because, there is a science behind being scared.

When this magnificent, critical, powerful machine otherwise known as your mind feels a looming threat it becomes very efficient in the face of danger. Your brain becomes hyper alert. Heart rate and blood pressure rises. Pupils dilate. Blood flows and the stream of glucose to the skeletal muscles increase. Breathing accelerates. Organs not perceived as vital in survival like the gastrointestinal system start to slow down.

In very basic terms when you are frightened you wake up, pay attention big time, breathe rapidly, that blood starts pumpin' and you get hype. But let me ask you something. Don't the exact same symptoms happen when you are at the very top of and are about to drop down on the amusement park roller coaster? Yes, grasshopper. Yes they do. When you are flying around in that cart screaming and getting bounced around you do wake up, pay attention big time, breathe rapidly while your blood is pumping and you do get hype. But you aren't scared. You are excited.

As you can imagine, the science of fear and physiology of the brain can get very complex. It also can be stripped down to become easily understandable. The more we can understand what and why something is happening to us the better we can manage it.

The prefrontal cortex part of our brain usually gets most the recognition. But the temporal lobe (located behind our temples) has an almond sized nuclei called the amygdala (uh-mig-duh-luh). We all have one and it is designed to keep us safe because it will activate our "fight or flight" responses. When necessary it also calls to the pituitary gland to release stress hormones.

We have a "thinking" part of our brain as well as an "emotional" part of our brain. The "thinking" brain gives immediate reports back to the "emotional" brain so you can act accordingly in any given situation. Or we should note that you will act "accordingly" as to how *your brain* perceives things in any given situation.

Let's use a gorilla as our example. If you are at a zoo and see a silverback gorilla in a cage or behind a glass wall your thinking brain identifies safety under the circumstances and you are chill. However if you were to encounter that same 5 foot, 400 pound gorilla baring it's teeth and knuckle walking while you are roaming through your neighborhood park, your thinking and emotional brain will quickly realize the danger and suddenly you qualify for your country's olympic track team.

As we can see, fear can be healthy. It alerts you, warns you, and in the right situation can save your life. But even in the unprecedented year 2020 (and hopefully beyond) it is pretty unlikely that you will not see that roaming gorilla in your non-post-apocalyptic park. Our overstimulated, primitively wired brains can work themselves up fairly quickly.

Back to that roller coaster. Your brain doesn't necessarily distinguish the difference between excitement and fear and it's all because of the one chemical your pituitary gland calls for the release of. Cortisol.

It's adrenaline. That's it. Pure adrenaline. It's not "frightened" adrenaline, and it's not "excited" adrenaline. It's simply adrenaline. The same, exact chemical is released when you are frightened as when you are excited. Once you understand this how you choose to use it is up to you.

> *"He who has overcome his fears will truly be free."* — Aristotle

In 2019 I attended one of many seminars which focused on personal growth. I was attending as an audience member as I believe that we all should never choose to stop growing.

At this one particular event I happened to know one of the presenters and I bumped into her moments before she was about to go onstage. Now I've read this person's books, I've seen her perform before literally tens of thousands, and she has been in the game of training years before I ever stepped up to a podium. So what she said to me after our initial greeting surprised me.

"Marc, I am so scared."

What? I was dumbfounded. This trainer doesn't get scared - not of training! Immediately I pulled her aside and felt compelled to not only support but remind this person what she already knew: that she was, is, and always will be one of the best.

"You are a beast!" I said. "People are excited and have come to see YOU. You are a total rockstar and you will slay this just like you always do."

Relief was the expression and I received a heartfelt "Thank you."

Moments later this speaker was introduced, took a deep breath and ran onto the stage to a welcoming, roaring, standing ovation. She did her thing and walked off that stage the same way she came on: to a roaring, standing ovation.

She controlled that emotion and used the adrenaline. She owned it.

You need to recognize and remember that you are in total control, so control it. Do not allow your mind to run rampant and actually bully you. Own it!

Next time you are about to step onto that stage, jump out of that airplane, walk into that room, or just do that thing, you may feel a pit in your stomach. Maybe your throat will start to close or your palms sweat. Maybe your heart will start pounding out of your chest and you'll shake. It has happened before so it could happen again. Next time it does, remember something important.

You are the boss. You are in control. This is where fear is a liar. There isn't an actual gorilla roaming, and lucky for that imaginary gorilla that it isn't because you are the real beast here.

Next time you are in a situation of "fear" suppress that small inner voice and let your bigger self out. DECIDE that you are EXCITED and not afraid. Why not? Your brain can't distinguish the difference. The cortisol can't distinguish the difference. Why should you try to distinguish the difference? Use this to your advantage.

Don't be afraid. Be excited. With a little courage and perspective this anti-fear technique could be just what the doctor ordered to turn your "frightening" situations into exciting ones. Now keep reading because coming up in the next key there is an idea that I'd really like you to entertain. We talked about being brave but it may be time to get just a little bit crazy.

## RANT #7

# SHHH

*"Thinking is the hardest work there is, which is the probable reason why so few engage in it."* — Henry Ford

**WE ARE ADDICTED** to noise. We have unknowingly been trained to be this way. The planet is the noisiest that it has ever been in the history of history. Because of this many of us have no idea how to be quiet. If many of us were to be quiet we wouldn't know what to do or how to handle it.

Tweets. Snaps. DMs. PMs. Email. Updates. Music. News. Schedules. Politics. Deadlines. Sports. Everything. It all seems so rushed, stressed, and obnoxiously in our faces.

Every single store, restaurant, or major public place we encounter has music. Why do you think the term "elevator music" was created? It's because for the 30 seconds that you will be on one it may have music playing that you apparently need to hear and can't live without.

Television is garbage. It's perpetual noise. It's constantly programming us with what we need, want, and must have while doing so using the undertone of fear being shoved down our throats. The internet is a circus of banners, ads, interruptions, and nonsense until you can actually connect to what you are looking for. Live events? One time I was at a professional sporting event when in between the chaos of announcements, commercialized marketing and nonstop hype, the person sitting next to me said "Wait. There's a game going on?"

We have become slaves to these little super computers known as our cell phones. Every ding, buzz, update, alarm, alert or text is a constant break in concentration. If you pay attention to the masses most people don't have the focus to interact with the person who is physically in front of them because of something more important that is commanding their attention from a handheld phone. It's crazy. Think about it. We drop everything that we are doing to answer it's beck and call. A ding or buzz stops us in our tracks from whatever conversation we are having or whatever task we are doing so we can see what that latest (important I'm sure) interruption is all about. In the process of writing that last sentence you've just read I had to stop and rewrite it. Why? That's right. A text just came in. You can't make this stuff up.

One year our family hosted a foreign exchange student from China who selected her American name to be Ruby. On one particular weeknight we took her to New York City as the obvious selection of "must see" places. It was jam-packed mobbed right in the heart of Times Square complemented by the total disarray of lights, colors, sounds, people, and traffic. We had to almost demand Ruby to pick her head up from her cell phone to look around. This child has already been to cities like Shanghai and Beijing that are double and triple the population of Midtown Manhattan. Ruby was bored. She was desensitized as she's seen it before on an even more thrilling, flashy, ADHD environment which made NYC seem like a church service.

It's all noise. It's never-ending commotion.

With all the nonstop disturbance how are we supposed to think? Here's the million dollar question. When was the last time you sat in a calm, peaceful manner and actually did think?

Henry Ford was the automotive titan who was bold enough to usher the world into a new way of living. History has shown that literal millenniums have passed where humans would travel by animal. Depending on the culture, camels, donkeys, elephants and the most advanced method of horse and buggy were the norm for transportation, work, and travel until the new phenomenon of the car. In the early 20th century Ford disrupted the past and put automobiles on the map.

In the Spring of 1928 a journal called "*The Forum*" interviewed Ford. He commented on how complex and rapid paced life had become with one of his now famous quotes: "But there is a question in my mind whether, with all this speeding up of our everyday activities, there is any more real thinking. **Thinking is the hardest work there is, which is the probable reason why so few engage in it.**" This was in the 1920s!

I have DJ'd for the last twenty years. My job is fun. It's hype and always a party. When I speak on my show or podcast I intend on making it full of spirit and energy. But when I'm off, I'm off. I don't always need music on my commute. I don't want a television on just making background noise. I like hearing nature in the morning doing it's thing when I wake up and it's peaceful.

It is vital for our mind and spirits to have silence. Stillness, tranquility, and calm allows one to listen better. We don't need constant disruption, distraction, and entertainment in our lives. Media serves enough of that constantly. We need to learn to become our own best advocate and shut out the noise. We need to create pockets of space where we can just be.

Let's start thinking more. Let's become more reflective. Let's be on purpose with creating and protecting our own environments where we make time to have quiet time. Let's be still. Let's get quiet. Let's take time to think. Like Henry said, it is hard work. Let's start choosing to be the ones who engage in it.

## KEY 7

# UNREALISTIC (GET CRAZY)

*"Here's to the crazy ones, the misfits, the rebels, the troublemakers, the round pegs in the square holes... the ones who see things differently—they're not fond of rules...because the ones who are crazy enough to think that they can change the world, are the ones who do."* — Steve Jobs

**DID YOU REALLY** pay attention to that quote? Steve Jobs said "The ones who are crazy enough to think that they can change the world, are the ones who do."

He didn't say "...the ones who are crazy enough but want to wait to see if other people approve first," or "...the ones who are crazy enough but will overthink it until they eventually do nothing." He definitely didn't speak of "...the ones who will take a poll with 50 of their unsuccessful friends who never had the guts to take a chance themselves." He spoke of rebels, round pegs in square holes, and ones who see things differently. His business started in a garage in the 1970s and now his legacy has turned MacBook Pro, iPhone, and beyond. Him. Listen to that guy.

I've unfortunately never met the man but I'm pretty sure Mr. Jobs wasn't talking about a "Frank Sinatra throwing broken television sets out of a Las Vegas hotel room window" kind of crazy. I'm thinking he meant "going against the grain, playing way beyond mediocre, and unleashing your special gift with laser beam focus" crazy. I'm certain we are talking about the type of "crazy" that shreds that word that I cannot stand. Realistic. I very much appreciate unrealistic. Most will blur crazy and unrealistic together. When you are "unrealistic" because you have a "crazy" idea that's everyone else setting a limit for what THEY think is possible—or impossible. The crazy and unrealistic is where the good stuff comes from. I'm going to get crazy right here because I want to share a very unrealistic story for you that I'm sure all of you delusional, square peg in round hole, rebel types will enjoy.

> *"Being realistic is the most commonly traveled road to mediocrity."* — Will Smith

Will Smith is amazing. He's been a top tv star, a Grammy Award winning, best-selling hip-hop artist, and one of the most paid leading men as a Hollywood actor in several top box office smashes. If you do some further digging, you will find this man has a freakish, obsessive, successful mindset.

He is a living example of a motivational speaker who actually walks the walk.

"Chill Will" (as some would call him from back in the early days when he was coming up in Philly) has some videos out there on the world wide web that will make you want to fight off evil aliens, save the whales, and start a movement that creates world peace—and that's all before you've had your breakfast. Mr. Smith has one in particular that always sticks out in my mind: his "delusional" video.

I'll save you the trouble of connecting to WiFi or finding a hot spot and quote him for you: "There's a certain delusional quality that all successful people have to have. You have to believe that something different than what has happened for the last fifty-million years of history—you have to believe that something different can happen."

I'm delusional. I think what I do is actually making the world better. I'm confident enough to believe that what I do makes a difference. I'm so unrealistic that I believe you can actually make a difference, too - even when you don't believe it. We need more people who strive to be beyond what is typical and traditional. Basic sucks.

Too many people are so "realistic" these days. Yawn. Boring. Realistic. Bleh.

We play it safe. We stay in the lines. We do what we're told. We don't want to ask questions or make waves.

Not make waves? Forget that noise. I say create a tsunami. Do you remember that guy who played it safe? Me neither.

I'm not saying be reckless, people. What I'm saying is if you want to create something that matters, or make a statement, or be the impact, then you have to rise above the norm. Creating something that matters, making a statement, and being "the" impact just doesn't grow on trees. It's rare.

Why is it rare? It's the same reason most kids won't raise their hand in class. It's exactly why many adults won't ask questions or speak up in a group or business meeting. You must step out from the crowd. And that "judge free" zone? It is a farce. It doesn't exist. Like it or not we are all (unfortunately) judging, and so many are worried about what will be thought of or said about them.

It's extreme with kids. I go into schools and literally promote that it is so important to be different. I ask them how boring would this place be if we all walked, talked and thought the same. How would it be if they all looked the same? What if they all looked like me? Bald with a face for radio. Creepy and odd (I know) but after some "eeew's" from the little kids and some "bruh's" from the older ones, they're pickin' up what I'm putting' down. I'm saying they get my point.

One time I was in a Catholic school and asked "How boring would it be if we all dressed the same?" Holy cow. That really happened. Nobody's perfect and we all can get better.

You weren't created to be mediocre. You didn't appear here by accident (regardless of what your parents told you). You definitely weren't created to be lazy and unproductive, although it's especially easy to be that way these days with so many options that can keep us distracted and comfortable.

You are special. One of a kind. There is not another you. You have imperfections. Own them. You are weird. Embrace it. You are purposely designed and wired differently than any other human being. Normal sucks and (let's face it) you are not normal. Congratulations. Hallelujah. High-five. Bang a gong, let's get it on.

In you there is that something. It's deep in there, too. No I'm not talking about your intestines, you crackpot. I'm talking about your "crazy" or whatever you want to call it. If you want to level up you need to go to that deep creative place inside of you, focus, and let that crazy out.

In the words of the immortal performer Prince: "Let's go crazy. Let's get nuts."

> "But we're never gonna survive, unless we get a little crazy." — Seal

Let's talk a little history. To be more specific—history regarding science and two of it's all time greatest minds.

Now hold on. Before you check out on me and start turning pages or scrolling, I want to get crazy for a second. I want to go on record as saying that science is ridiculously fascinating and history is undeniably mesmerizing. Yes, I know. Crazy. Well let's just say that they would be fascinating and mesmerizing if they were actually taught that way.

When you tell me that the Iroquois main trade was tobacco and corn for wampum from the tribes of the east, I want to bang my face into a wall because you're boring me to tears. And what the heck is wampum anyway?

Now, when you get real with it and tell me that the end of the movie "*Braveheart*" didn't actually explain what happened to Scotland's own William Wallace you have my attention. Spoiler alert. I'm about to ruin *Braveheart* for you. I'm dead serious. If you haven't seen *Braveheart* yet just jump to the next paragraph. When you tell me that 1995's violent "R" rated *Braveheart* went soft because they didn't want to show you that Wallace's torture incorporated him being strangled and released while still alive, emasculated, torn to pieces with his bowels burned before him, beheaded, and cut into four parts while his preserved head (dipped in tar) was placed on a pike at London Bridge, now I am fascinated and mesmerized. You dig?

Back to the the history of who are believed to be two of the greatest minds ever. Greatest? Yes. Normal? No. Crazy? Possibly.

Nikola Tesla was extraordinary. He has been referred to as "the man that invented the twentieth century." Is he the creator of the Tesla car? No, but the "Sorcerer Of Lightning" created the high voltage "AC" or alternating current which powers everything from the Tesla car engine, to your headphones, and even your cable modem.

As the United States was in the process of growing and recovering from a Civil War, Nikola Tesla was too busy to notice. After his move from Serbia to the U.S. he was more focused on changing the planet and creating some of his credited three hundred patents! AC (think of battery charged), wireless power, x-ray, radio waves, remote control, robotics, and lasers are just to name a few of the life changing inventions this genius had. When I DJ, what would my dance floor look like without Nikola's inventions of lasers and methods of harnessing light. Thank you, science. Thank you, Tesla. You literally made me "lit." Tesla basically gets the credit for at least eighty percent of all technology that we have today. Powerful. Brilliant. Amazing!

However, my man was far from "normal." I'd say borderline crazy. Oops. I did it again. Too much? Is "eccentric" better? You decide. It is rumored he would curl his toes exactly one hundred times a day. He would eat dinner every night at 8:10 p.m. Sharp. Hygiene was in question, his best friends were pigeons, and he bragged on sleeping two hours a night. He had visions, memorized full books, and he was quoted as stating "The feeling is constantly growing on me that I had been the first to hear the greeting of one planet to another." Zoinks!

Albert Einstein? Scientist. Physicist. Genius. Phenom.

Albert hated school. It is rumored that he wasn't even good at school. You read that correctly. One of the most brilliant minds and greatest scientists this world has ever seen was not good in an organized educational setting. I suppose that's where one of his famous quotes stemmed from when he said "Everybody is a genius. But if you judge a fish by its ability to climb a tree, it will live its whole life believing that it is stupid."

Without going into an entire life bio on the man he created, got noticed, and finally broke through in the "miracle year" of 1905 while writing one of his several papers in which his "Theory Of Relativity" was born. I am not going to even pretend that I am somewhat close to a science buff, but the idea is energy is equal to mass times the speed of light squared, or famously put "$E = mc2$." Understand? I don't. But that doesn't matter. What does matter is that he changed the game, how we now view how science and physics intertwines with the universe, and most importantly how we think. Forever.

Einstein became more than relevant. He was "the" game changer and became an overnight celebrity. Prior to his first trip to America the *New York Times* headline read "EINSTEIN'S COMING!" More than 15,000 people swarmed the docks of Manhattan—to see a physicist! As radiant and resourceful as Albert Einstein was, is it accurate to say he had a little bit of cuckoo going on?

The Nobel Prize Winner was married more than once. I get it. It's the roaring twenties. No big deal, bro. Right? Eh, you didn't let me finish. That second marriage was to his mistress who was also (drum roll, please) … his cousin. Yuck. Allow me to continue.

He hated socks. He was a known pacifist but encouraged US President FDR to have a nuclear bomb. He turned down the offer to be the second President of Israel, was an obsessive smoker, and apparently very, very sloppy.

Want to see a train wreck? I can direct you to a picture that looks like someone dumped a filing cabinet, ransacked it for spare change, and made it look like an unexpected earthquake happened. This picture was taken the day after Einstein died in 1955, and it was of his desk. Google "Einstein's Office." Go ahead. I'll wait.

> *"My psychiatrist told me I was crazy and I said I want a second opinion. He said okay, you're ugly too."* — Rodney Dangerfield

They're all whacked. One of America's Founding Fathers - Benjamin Franklin - signed the Constitution, engineered the U.S. Postal system, created everything from bifocals to the lightning rod (so your home won't burn down), and is currently on that $100 bill in your pocket just to name a few of his massive achievements. I'm joking. I know you don't have a $100 bill in your pocket. The rest? All true and then some.

It is also said that Benjamin Franklin would sit naked in front of open windows and take "air baths" to "prevent sickness." He drank wine and beer like a college kid at a frat house on a Thursday night, wrote a paper titled "*Fart Proudly*," and lived in a London home where 1,200 human bones were discovered. Talk about skeletons in the closet.

It is believed that Sir Isaac Newton created Calculus. You can thank him for years of failing grades and anxiety. You can also thank him for the law of gravitation. Remember the story of the guy who had an apple fall out of a tree onto his head, and then he went on to advance the world of science? Yeah, him. This sage was at the forefront of the scientific revolution of the seventeenth century. He needs to be in the conversation when we mention great minds like a Tesla and an Einstein.

It is also believed that he believed once he created the "Philosopher's Stone" that he could transmute metals into gold and grant human beings immortality. Welp, he died. So that's that. Newton also was suggested to be a cranky insomniac who hated Catholics, women, Catholic women, and while trying to crack what he believed was a "Bible Code" had predicted in his writings from 1704 that the end of the world would be no later than the year 2060. That sucks because I'll only be 89 and I have high hopes of being a centenarian. Thank you modern medicine?

Howard Hughes (American business tycoon, inventor, filmmaker, etc) refused to leave his screening room for months while living on milk and chocolate, and relieving himself in empty containers. Gross.

It has been documented that Winston Churchill who was one of the greatest wartime leaders of the twentieth century really enjoyed parading around. Naked.

President Andrew Jackson loved gun fights - especially duels. King of France Charles VI otherwise known as Charles "The Mad" ran around his castle howling and chasing people but didn't want to be touched—because he of course—was a glass wolf that could shatter. And Stonewall Jackson of the Civil War had a full burial ceremony in which he was alive and present. How? Because the ceremony was for his amputated left arm, you silly goose. Presidents, generals, kings. Kings? How about the "King Of Pop" Michael Jackson? He had a chimpanzee named Bubbles. But, he also wore a face mask before they were the in thing, so maybe he knew more than we realize. It seems the bigger the name, the more the crazy. I rest my case.

Now is history and science still boring? It's fascinating, right? My point is maybe guys like Steve Jobs and Will Smith are onto something with this crazy, delusional thing. Clearly some of the biggest names in history were. I'm not suggesting that you need to pee in bottles, marry your cousin, or think you are a glass wolf in order to be successful. I am saying that what Steve Jobs said may be true: "The ones who are crazy enough to think that they can change the world, are the ones who do." Maybe it's time to start getting a little crazy.

Realistic is not only boring, it will give you exactly what you requested from it. Common, basic, and the very polar opposite of fantastic. Remember that it is not bad, but good which is the enemy of great. If you seek "great," do yourself a favor and start getting unrealistic.

## RANT #8

# HUMILITY

*"I live for the applause...Live for the way that you cheer and scream for me. The applause, applause, applause." — "Applause" by Lady Gaga*

**WHEN THE CORONAVIRUS** Pandemic of 2020 arrived on a global scale, it came swiftly. With it, it brought a barrage of emotions ranging from fear, anger, sadness, and uncertainty. One particular virtue that it dished out to everyone was widely overlooked. This state of consciousness was dealt with by each one of us in one way or another, whether we realized it or not.

We dealt with humility.

We all came to a place where everything that we knew as familiar stopped. It didn't matter how much money was in the bank account, what title was attached to the ego that showboated it, or what past achievements were earned. The bubble of comfort was burst.

Suddenly, we were all given limits. Limits were put on where we could go, what we could do, and how much we could have. Regardless if you were on welfare or were a multimillionaire, your store shelves were stocked—or lacking just the same. You could only buy two of each item, and eventually you'll need toilet paper too, just like everyone else. Maybe you could get your hands on some, but maybe not. You were reduced to rationing.

The greatest musical performers had no one to perform to. When they did, it was virtual. There would be no applause. Athletes couldn't be athletic and compete. When they could, there would be no cheers, no jeers and no emotion. The reverb was silence. Speakers had no crowds to speak to, leaders had nowhere to lead anyone, and everything came to a pause.

The great became inessential. We all became the same. Everyone was equal. There were no special privileges. If you tapped into your feelings, what you would feel was mortality. If you listened carefully you could hear the universe whispering to remind us all of just how fragile we really are.

The dictionary defines humility as "the state of being humble." Both humility and humble have origin from the Latin word humilis, meaning "low." In a "look at me" culture where so much is superficial, and in a world where sports, music, movies, games, and the day to day is stacked with boasting and arrogance, isn't humility refreshing?

You've read earlier in this book how Napoleon Hill wrote in his book (*Think And Grow Rich*): "The Great Depression was a blessing in disguise. It reduced the whole world to a new starting point that gave everyone a new opportunity." The book of Proverbs tells us "When pride comes, then comes disgrace, but with humility comes wisdom."

I believe a hard look in the mirror, a deep self check and a nice, fresh cup of humility should not only be welcomed but essential for our souls. It's needed. Sometimes you have to take a step back in order to leap three steps forward. In times of silence and submissiveness, if you view it as a negative I believe that you are looking at it wrong. Be thankful for the moments of humility, for the lesson that comes with it can be our greatest teacher.

## KEY 8

# GRATITUDE (HAPPY TO BE HERE)

*"Enough' is a feast."* — Buddhist proverb

**I LOVE THANKSGIVING.** That's primarily because I love all things involved with it. Food? Love it. Family? Love them. Football? Yes, please. Fun? That's what I am—a big, fat ball of fun. Although I love Thanksgiving, I'm pretty sure that everyone around me doesn't necessarily love *me* on Thanksgiving, more specifically on Thanksgiving morning.

Something else that I love is being a DJ. For the better half of almost a decade now I have been the DJ for our county's yearly 5k "Turkey Trot." It takes place at Kottmeyer Stadium (Home of Downingtown West High School) where the Whippets from West and the Cougars from Downingtown East alternate home field advantage each week during the football season.

Years ago when I was initially asked to DJ the event, I said that I would in exchange for my wife and kids having access to run in it. Access was granted, but to this day I'm still waiting for my wife and kids to actually run in it. I guess it was a gift that they really didn't ask for, just like if I were to buy my wife an NFL jersey for Mother's Day.

Each year I wake up at 4, leave at 5, arrive at 5:30 and by 6am I am once again rocking' the trot with bodacious beats and dope jamz. So why do I say people around me don't necessarily love me on Thanksgiving? Because I'm dropping those beats and jamz with not my own, but the stadium's loudspeakers. The entire town knows when I get in the stadium - and trust me - nobody wants to hear "Footloose" at 6am, especially not at 6 am on Thanksgiving morning.

One time I received a text from someone who wasn't at the run, but lives a quarter of a mile away from the stadium. It read "Can you play 'Shut Up And Dance?'" Yuck. Requests. From across town.

But "turkey day" (even though I don't eat turkey) is my jam. There's usually a point sometime throughout the day when we all here in the US will take a moment and stop to reflect on all the things that we are grateful for.

Although the holiday itself is a great sentiment and can create a time when we may actually stop and appreciate, quite frankly everyday should be and can be Thanksgiving. Each new day should start with appreciation of not just what we have, but all that we are, and all that is around us. We've been blessed by the best and live in great abundance.

In a time where we are in a world of social media where it's easy to compare everyone's best performance with our own worst practice, we can quickly forget how amazing our day to day can be, and how grateful we should be for it.

> *"This is a wonderful day. I've never seen this one before"* — Maya Angelou

What's another one of my favorite days you ask? Well, you didn't, but I'm gonna tell you anyway. It's my birthday. I feel like a superhero on my birthday. The funny thing is I didn't even do anything to deserve it. My mom did. I simply just showed up. Regardless, you should feel like a million bucks on your birthday. It's your special day to celebrate you.

In saying that, I felt bad for so many kids that had birthdays during the quarantine timeframe. What I thought about was what they were missing out on. I could only imagine how it would feel to not be able to gather with family and friends when it should be a time to party and enjoy.

Then one day some friends of mine invited me to a drive by for their fifteen year old son's birthday. It was nice to be thought of enough to be invited, but again I couldn't help but feel bad for the boy. Not knowing what to expect, we gathered up as a family and looked to join the "festivities."

Now at that time I (like most other people) have never had the reason or opportunity to be part of a "drive by" for a birthday celebration, so I seriously had no idea what it would be like. In my mind the whole thing was pretty awkward.

Then we got there. We met up at the local fire department's parking lot and I was surprised to see how many people showed. Not only did they show, but as more vehicles piled in, more and more pockets of people knew each other. We were parked a few spaces down from friends of ours. Even though we all stayed in our vehicles windows were getting rolled down, conversations were happening, and the air was filled with laughter. Then it hit me that this was actually...fun? Weird? Yes. Different? Yes. A party? Actually...yes!

When it was time to roll (literally), we all followed one of the big rig fire trucks single file style. Police blocked off the major roads at intersections so what looked like a funeral procession turned celebration was uninterrupted by local traffic. As we turned down the side street to approach the birthday boys' house, anticipation was mounting. It was actually exciting!

Then the commotion started. Fire truck sirens were blaring, horns were honking, music was playing, and the birthday boy was smiling. Wide. One by one as each one of us rolled by the front of their yard with signs, waves, and high spirits, we were all part of and created a once in a lifetime memory.

I couldn't believe how fun and quick the whole event was. What hit me as soon as the whole shindig was a wrap was the thought that I went into this feeling sorry for the boy. I was viewing him as someone who "had" to have an isolated birthday party, when in fact this lucky boy "got" to have a birthday parade! That's awesome! Can I have a parade for my birthday?

Perspective is so powerful. We are masters of taking things for granted. You don't like where you live? You live somewhere. Don't like what you drive? You can drive. Don't like your job? You make a living. There is always someone, somewhere who has it worse than you.

Before we had all this technology, in the 1990's I had a few surgeries on my knee ending with major reconstruction. It was a terrible process. For the longest time it became very...inconvenient. But, inconvenient compared to what? Later in life before passing away my father spent years of being bedridden. I bet if his body allowed him, he would have jumped (literally) at the chance to chose my "inconvenience" over his. I've never complained about my knee (or knees) being as bad as they are again. They hurt, but I can walk.

As we are so quick to be half empty, we need to stop and be thankful and more appreciative for so many of those things that we *do* have.

> "When eating the fruit, remember the one who planted the tree" — Vietnamese Proverb

I find that gratitude is a most overlooked necessity on many levels. It's underestimated and yet so powerful for how it can shape our life. Ultimately we love the idea of having gratitude because deep down inside we know that we should have it. It feels right to acknowledge someone or something that we should be thankful for.

There is a difference between being thankful and being comfortable. Comfortable suffocates. Thankful is important. You can be hungry and desire more while not getting lazy and yet stay thankful for what you have. Be thankful for who you are, where you are, what you have, and most importantly what you can give. Being thankful for all of those people and all of your life experiences—even the less desirable ones—is absolutely important as they have shaped who you have become, who you can be, and who you can teach and lift up because of them.

Be thankful for your sight, your hearing, your home, your family, your circle, your livelihood, your problems that make you stronger. Rejoice in this very day that you were given and the possibility of God willing - having another - and a better one tomorrow. While Steve Jobs was giving a commencement speech he noted that when he was 17 he heard a quote that said "If you live each day as if it were your last, someday you'll most certainly been right." Why chose to live your days in fear, anger, regret and anxiousness when you can chose gratitude?

Do yourself a favor and create a "gratitude journal." Each night before bed write three to five things that you were thankful for that day. Yes even on the rough day during the tough times. What a change you'll start to see in your life as you will have an attitude of gratitude. And (as you've heard before) attitude is everything.

> "The more thankful I became, the more my bounty increased. That's because — for sure — what you focus on expands. When you focus on the goodness in life, you create more of it." — Oprah Winfrey

I say all the time that I believe opportunity creates opportunity. Motion creates motion. DJing, speaking, authoring books led me to my next step of podcasting and becoming a radio host for my show the *"Get Up Power Hour."*

The radio broadcast and the podcast both are like drinking out of the firehouse with a high energy, swing for the fences, take no prisoners kind of attitude. I absolutely love having the platform and opportunity where I can share my thoughts and showcase others who inspire the masses.

There were times while dropping my podcast (*Get Up Podcast*) that I had only one person listening. Me. Then there would be two or three listeners. You know, my wife and my mom. Yikes. There were times at the station during live radio broadcasts where we would come out of a commercial break and "open up the phone lines so you can weigh in" and…crickets. But you just keep on punching. Or you should.

Why? For starters I am thankful. So thankful. I am genuinely thrilled just for being able to have the opportunity to be an on-air host and have a radio show or a podcast. It's a dream come true. I was making "shows" in my bedroom with cassette tapes and a boom box back in 1985 when I was a kid. Now I can go live and maybe, just maybe I'm making a difference in somebody's life and brightening up their day. That fuels me.

Next, I can't explain what it feels like to have sponsors. These sponsors are big companies, people with ideas, or especially small businesses who need to be careful where every penny goes. The moment they take those hard earned dollars and say that they believe in me or my message, it is truly humbling. The bet and they bet on me. That is a responsibility of helping them grow that is something that I am always happy to oblige. We lift each other up.

Finally, it isn't always about the results or the end game. It's about the process and the journey. If you had initial, instantaneous, never ending success, how can you actually enjoy it? How can you be excited with the overwhelming joy that winning brings if you haven't ever lost? "Failure" or struggle is a tremendous teacher and helps you grow with the lesson it is showing you. Be thankful for it. I had many rejections with trying to secure my first ever book signing for my first ever book "*Get Up.*" I was laughed at. Who do you think was laughing when my first actual signing came to fruition packing the hotel room with people who stood in line that literally wrapped around to the outside lobby? I told you of the podcasts that I released (which are all still out there) when nobody cared. The comments and texts that I receive from sometimes across the world of someone telling me that the one they did listen to changed their life, changes mine. The times when I "opened up the lines" for callers on a radio show when no one was calling in made the moments that much sweeter for the times when the call volume literally took the station's phone lines down. We broke the radio.

I appreciate all of it. That perspective of an attitude of gratitude attracts success, abundance, and ultimately more to be thankful for. There is an unwritten law with an unseeable frequency which decrees what you focus on multiplies and attracts more. So let me ask you: got gratitude?

Let me ask you one more thing. How could I publish a book about lighting up darkness if I didn't have any mention of gratitude? I couldn't. So ending this quick chapter I just want you to know that I'm thankful for you, the gift that you are to this crazy place, and for you taking the time to consider all of these thoughts. Now let's keep this spirit of appreciation as our foundation while we move forward. And make no mistake, we are moving forward.

## RANT #9

# FORGIVE

*"Every saint has a past while every sinner has a future."* — Oscar Wilde

**LIVE BY THE** sword, die by the sword, right? I know that you know that those who live in glass houses shouldn't throw stones. I'm not preaching that all of us are not perfect because you already know that. I am reminding you that every single one of us screw up and unfortunately sometimes screw up big time. Remember an amateur built the ark and professionals built the Titanic.

It is imperative for us to come full circle and forgive. People have done us wrong. We have crossed others. I know that sometimes this is something we push away so we don't even have to deal with it. I understand. It's complicated, messy, and very, very ugly. It gets dark. It wasn't supposed to happen and nobody else would get it.

It's time. It's time to quiet your mind. Soften your heart. Show some mercy.

This one is a tough one though. I want you to forgive the one who may need that forgiveness the most. That person who hurt you the most and constantly lets you down needs some amnesty.

I want you to forgive you.

You are a beautiful mess. The good stuff, the bad stuff—it is going to be alright. There is not another one like you and we are all a work in progress from start to finish. We learn. We change. We grow.

I want you to know that the darkest thought in your mind is temporary and fleeting. You body of work is unique and you need another chance. You actually deserve one.

Forgive. Forgive yourself. You will be with you forever and you weren't made or expected to be perfect. You are expected to get better. So give yourself another chance. You've made a mistake? So did everyone else on the planet from Adam and Eve to Kanye and Kim.

Buy yourself flowers. Scream into a pillow. Treat yourself to ice cream. Hit a heavy bag. Smash a tennis racket into the mattress. Run a mile or have a date with you and splurge on yourself at your favorite restaurant. Tell yourself you are sorry and repair.

I'm thankful for you. You are special. You matter. You are needed. It is time to heal up, get up, and get ready for the next chapter of not what you are going to do wrong, but what you are going to do great. Forgive.

## KEY 9

# FAITH
# (THE POWER OF BELIEF)

*"(What's So Funny 'Bout) Peace, Love, and Understanding"* — Elvis Costello

IN 2019 I found myself back in Northern New Jersey. You know, the part of Jersey that keeps getting mistaken by the rest of the world for New York. The Meadowlands? Exit 16? Rutt's Hut? Eh, never mind.

The important part is that I was walking into a high school to speak at an assembly. I was the author of "*Get Up (Encouraging You To Attack Life)*" and I was coming to blow the doors off the place. My intent was to inject some mindset and offer some uplifting, positive messages for the kids who—let's face it—in today's world don't always have the opportunities to hear messages like that. As I always do whenever I speak to any group, I arrive with purpose. That day wasn't any different as I walked into there *knowing* without a doubt that I was going to change somebody's life.

As I was cleared by security and met by the counselor who was escorting me to where I would speak, we had the usual banter as we continued through the hallways. I usually hear familiar questions like "How was your trip," or "Can I get you anything," but regardless of conversation I am always focused on the upcoming task.

"So, uh, I read your book," the counselor said.

I responded with "Oh, thank you. That's great!" This is typically my response when I'm told something like this, and it's authentic. I truly feel that it is "great" anytime someone takes time and gives energy towards something that I have created. It's humbling. What wasn't typical was the next question that I was about to be asked. I'll have to admit that it caught me off guard as I wasn't expecting it and haven't heard it before.

"Yeah" she said. "Your book. It was good. Really good. But I noticed in the beginning you mentioned a few things that…well, it's just…you aren't going to talk about God or anything like that, are you?"

"I'm sorry? I'm not quite sure I under—"

"Because," she interrupted. "We're a public school and all. So, were you planning on talking about God?"

"Did you want me to talk about God?"

"Oh no," she said while shaking her head waving her hands in front of her. "We're looking to just have you come in and speak, you know, about your book. Talk about some of the stories you have in there that may help the kids and all."

"Ok," I said. "You're sure? Because if you want me to I don't have a problem with talking about—"

"No, no, no," she interrupted a bit nervously. "Just talk about your book. Please."

We reached the end of the hallway near the auditorium and no other words were spoken between us. Awkward would be an understatement.

On that day with those kids I didn't talk about God. And for the record, typically when I speak at events (unless I'm asked about my faith) I usually don't. To have someone specifically urge me not to is interesting. As a matter of fact, it's a problem.

To be clear I have zero issues with speaking on my core beliefs. I don't routinely publicly talk about faith or my faith in particular as it's simply not what I'm usually being booked to speak about. But, I'm going to speak about it here.

> *"Tell the truth, work hard, and come to dinner on time."* — former U.S. President Gerald R. Ford

Every year my wife Christina and I take our kids to a different city that has a NFL Team. That would be the "National Football League" for anyone reading outside of the U.S. No, I don't mean soccer. You know. Football. American Football. The New York Giants. The Denver Broncos. The New England Patriots. The Cleveland Browns. The Cleveland who? Never mind.

Like I was saying...each year we pick a new team, buy our tickets, load up on their apparel, and plan our trip. I call it the "Diaper Tour." We started when the kids were in diapers and we'll probably end when I'm in diapers because there just are so many teams.

We make it about more than just a football game. It's an adventure. The travel is *usually* fun (have you tried to travel with your entire family lately? "Dad, she's looking at me.") and we make at least a long weekend out of it. One thing I focus on when researching travel plans is to make it a "When In Rome" approach. No we don't want to go to the local science museum, Dunkin' Donuts, or whatever other generic thing you can throw our way. Green Bay has a way different vibe than Miami, which has a different feel than Houston, which (culturally speaking) is the opposite side of the planet from the New York Jets. I want my family to taste it all. It's a pretty great experience.

On our ninth year of travel we decided to visit the Cincinnati Bengals. That was a fun one. The city was clean, the people were friendly and we packed in as much as we could for the few days we were there. We toured the Christian Creation Museum, ate Skyline Chili until we were delighted and uncomfortable, and even ventured to Northern Kentucky to try out the "Ark Encounter." It's the actual sized replica of Noah's Ark—what an attraction!

Game day was a fantastic experience for me as the trip planner because other than the Baltimore Ravens (year number three), this was the first time I secured a hotel that was in walking distance of the field. You could see "Paul Brown Stadium" just 3 blocks away. Fabulous.

Before and after the game we walked amongst all the Bengals faithful. We had a blast at the game when they won and then we traipsed back to our hotel with intentions to hit the indoor rooftop pool. Being the inexperienced out-oftowner that I was, I overindulged and purchased a bunch of "Cheese Coneys" which we couldn't finish at the game. I absolutely despise when food gets wasted so instead of tossing them I decided they were coming back to our mini fridge at the hotel.

What's that? What's a Cheese Coney? How dare you.

A Cheese Coney is this perfect train wreck of a mini all beef hotdog on a mini bun. On top of the hot dog is a more than necessary amount of all beef chili with what would seem like forty-seven pounds of shredded cheese. I realize right now all of my health and wellness friends are wincing, but it's the best potential heart attack you can ever have. If you order it throw away your detox plans for a day or two after selecting this masterpiece because you cannot eat just one. I have not eaten meat for years now but when I did this a was pretty marvelous experience.

Getting another year of our tour in the books I felt like an accomplished father as I trailed our family watching them all walking back. My daughter Jayda was happy and occupied with herself, oblivious to the fact that even in "smaller cities" that aren't New York you should still keep your guard up. My wife had her "I Just Want To Get Back To The Hotel And I Am Done With All Of These People" march, while my two boys Kane and Harrison were busy irritating and knocking the snot out of each other right there in the streets of Cincinnati. Ah, life was good.

As this was a Sunday afternoon turning evening many of the stores we were passing were closed. Some were vacant. One vacant store in particular had a bunch of cardboard boxes and trash bags piled in front of it and it happened to catch my eye. It wasn't the store. It wasn't the trash. It was what was laying tucked in between the trash that got my attention. It was a human being.

As the Christmas lights of early December hung everywhere this man was laying there in between bags dressed in heavy layers of clothes to keep warm. Simply reacting I started walking towards him as my soul pulled me towards this man. With my family moving up the street unaware (and clearly not concerned) that I was missing from the pack, I stopped and extended my arm holding the styrofoam carton of food from the Stadium.

The man looked up at me with a degree of embarrassment in his eyes. Without hesitation, he took the box, nodded, and thanked me. I couldn't help but notice how young he was. Maybe he was in his mid twenties. Maybe a little older. He had a full head of brown hair and a boyish face that had much life in it. I just told him that he was welcome and I started back up the street.

Then something odd happened. Just as my soul pulled me towards him initially, after about half a block of steps from leaving him my spirit stirred me. It stirred me enough to turn me around and head straight back to that pile of trash and the man who sat underneath it. There was an odd feeling that I hadn't experienced before. For no good reason that I could explain, I was angry. I wasn't personally angry with him. It was almost as if I was the chosen messenger who was going to deliver a message.

By the time I made it back to him he had already ripped open the box and was tearing up the Coneys. Surprise was the look he had on his face when after about two minutes I returned to stand over him saying nothing. What did I want? Did I need directions? Did I want my hot dogs back? He froze mid chew and we locked eyes.

I had no agenda. I had nothing planned to say. We just starred at each other for I'm sure what was the most uncomfortable twenty seconds that either of us have ever experienced in our lives. Then it just came out of me.

"Look man, you are too young for this."

He continued to stare.

"God has a purpose for you," I said. "You have more than a lifetime of living to do and sitting here feeling sorry for yourself isn't living. It's existing. Get back on your feet and start living."

His eyes drifted from mine and he slowly bowed his head. A ray of shame reigned over him.

I just stood there. I didn't know what was next. I had nothing else to say. That was it. That was the message.

Carefully he raised his head and looked up at me. He nodded as if he got it. Message received. Loud and clear. Special delivery for him and he signed for it. We actually bumped fists then I turned and walked away.

It suddenly occurred to me—I'm standing on a side street in Cincinnati yelling at a homeless man. I am seconds away from spending the night in an Ohio jail cell. Even worse I could go viral on TikTok. I can see it now. "Hey kids, where's dad? Let's get the wifi password and find out."

So many times we create our own prisons for ourselves. These prisons can come in all different forms. Often we forget that we actually have the very key to let ourselves out.

I never saw that man again. I have no idea as to where he is, what he's doing, if he did or did not decide to change his circumstances—no clue. Maybe he went on to do some tremendous things. Maybe he picked himself up and started his own charity to help others who are in need. Maybe he creates a ring of safe shelters for those in need. Maybe he's still laying in a heap of trash consumed by his own issues. I don't know. Maybe he's reading this now. Crazy, right? Maybe, just maybe he thinks about that random guy who appeared to him on some random Sunday afternoon punching him in the gut with a message that he needed to hear.

Your actions, OUR actions have effects on people for the positive or negative. I've talked about it before - that energy. Use it! And be aware. You may have no clue how you can effect someone - especially someone who may be in dire need - just at that right time when they know they need it and are ready to receive it. And what if they're not?

Can you think of a time that a teacher, coach, parent, or somebody has given you guidance or instruction in your life when you weren't open or ready? Did you look back and appreciate it differently? Did you possibly realize that it's the way to go and that you could pass that wisdom onto others? It's never a waste.

Be receptive, friends. We are here for a purpose and I believe it is bigger than us. I believe it is to lift each other up, not to tear each other down. Listen to your inner voice. That intuition? It's not an accident. It's a message. Be the messenger.

When you are in times of struggling because (as we all do) you hear that small voice of doubt, just know—BELIEVE—that God didn't bring you this far only to bring you this far. Have faith!

> *"Faith is taking the first step even when you can't see the whole staircase."* — Dr. Martin Luther King Jr.

I want to speak life over you. There is no doubt that the world we live in can be evil and dark. But, at the same time there is so much beauty that has been created for us. The days we walk in are both uncertain and unprecedented times, but there is still so much to hope for and believe in.

In some of the worst moments and ugliest tragedies that we have lived through, we have seen love, hope and faith stand tall and unwavering, bringing us together with that human connectivity that deep down binds us all.

Down to the heart of it we aren't Democrats or Republicans. We aren't hunters or vegans. We aren't blue or white collar. We're people who instinctively need and want to be loved. All those dividing lines were learned, but what we have built into our core is innate. We need to be loved. We need to love. We need community. We need connectivity. Nobody wants to be or should be alone. We need each other. And, we need to keep the faith.

This world is really good at trying to put your light out, but never lose that spark. Stay faithful to the fact that you have a purpose. Don't be a victim and hope. Go on the offense and KNOW that you were created for bigger things than what you are doing now. Understand that you can be the difference maker, and that can start right now. There is no better time. Most shoot low, so aim high. Realize the ones who take the leap of faith find greater rewards with what's on the other side.

I hope this book was more than just a book for you. I hope it was an experience. Every good book has only bits and pieces of it that is ultimately remembered by it's reader. As you move forward and into that scary unknown proposition of what we call the future, my wish for you is that you carry the theme and message of this read in your heart.

Mind your mindset. Level up that attitude. Show courage. Learn to have vision. Stay disciplined. Get motivated. Be unrealistic. Have gratitude. And, keep the *faith*.

Walk boldly now. You've been called to light up the darkness.

# I BELIEVE

**I BELIEVE IN** you. I believe in me, too. I believe we don't have to compete. I believe we should lift each other up. I believe there is enough sunshine for all of us to get a tan. I always have.

I believe they try to make it hard for us. But, I believe we are stronger than our problems. I believe we can always rise above. I believe we should lift each other up.

I believe in our elderly and the living history that they are. I believe their stories are the best. I believe we should not just spend time with them, but let them know how appreciated they are.

I believe in the children. I believe that they will do better than we did. I believe we need to let them know how great they are. I believe there really isn't a bad kid. I believe the kid who acts the worst needs to be loved the most.

I believe our past doesn't define us, but I believe it can motivate us. I believe the good old days weren't always that good. I believe the future isn't as terrible as they want us to think. I believe we can predict the future we want, because we can create the future we want. I believe we should lift each other up.

I believe God gave us two ears and one mouth so we can listen twice as much as we speak. I believe we need to hear more and talk less. I believe we need to be more patient. I believe we should laugh much, much more. I believe it's okay to not have all the answers, and I believe it's even better to admit it when you don't. I believe people will trust and respect you more when you are honest like that. I believe admitting your weakness is a strength and boasting your strength is a weakness.

I believe you need to take better care of yourself. I believe you should love yourself. You are special. I believe that sometimes you do need a break. I believe we need to take better care of each other, too. I believe we should lift each other up.

I believe there is a time when you need to fight. I believe if you do need to fight, you should do it in a way where no one will ever want to make you have to fight again. But, I believe you should talk first. I believe in the power of communication. I believe in being open. I believe in being kind. I believe in understanding. I believe in the benefit of the doubt. I believe in best intentions.

I believe we have both wasted precious time. I believe we can make the most of our time now. I believe in now.

When now ends, I believe the end is a new beginning.

I believe we need to lift each other up. I believe we are going to win.

I believe in you.

# ABOUT THE AUTHOR

**MARC HAYFORD IS** a two time best-selling author, inspirational speaker, podcaster, and radio host. With a no-nonsense, high energy delivery Hayford's mission statement encourages you to play all out and showcases a higher vision of not what is probable, but what is possible.

Marc gives motivational talks and is an author for his two previous best-selling books "*Get Up (Encouraging You To Attack Life)*" and "*365 Days Of Encouraging You To Attack Life*" which each hit #1 topping Amazon's "Self Help" charts! Hayford is a former professional wrestling referee, a DJ for his own company, a veteran of the US armed forces, as well as a head football coach for middle school. He has been featured, interviewed and speaks on many platforms such as radio, television, and podcasts including his own daily podcast "*GET UP*" and his current radio show the "*GET UP POWER HOUR!*"

For more information, to order books, to schedule a speaking event or connect with Marc personally, please go to

WWW.MARCHAYFORD.COM

Made in the USA
Middletown, DE
24 July 2020